INTRODUCTION

This book explains the proper concepts and strategies used for playing pot-limit and no-limit poker, as given by two top-flight professional players. The forms of poker commonly played at this type of betting structure are thoroughly discussed. These include hold'em, Omaha, seven-card stud, and several varieties of lowball. The three basic poker types of straight high, high-low split, and low are all covered.

The vast majority of top-level poker players prefer pot-limit and no-limit poker. There is greater opportunity to obtain a nice result through the exercise of skill, because good decisions offer a greater reward, and bad decisions invoke a more severe penalty. There is much more that a good player can do to triumph over weaker opponents. Even though many of these stronger players actually spend more time playing limit poker, this is only because those games often are more readily available, and the caliber of opposition weaker.

But until now, there has been very little material available to a player interested in big-bet poker (our name for pot-limit and no-limit betting). The wealth of information within this book radically changes this situation. Many strategies used by the top players are revealed for the first time in these pages. Frankly, it will be very hard for a player who has not read this book to compete successfully against those who have profited by reading it. The authors hope that big-bet poker will undergo a new surge of popularity as a result of their efforts.

If you are going to try and popularize a form of poker, it is necessary to tell people how to play it properly. Revealing important information reduces the advantage of the good player, but at least he will have a game to play in. When you slaughter people practically every time they play, they are not going to stick around. On balance, we feel we are doing the better players a favor by promoting big-bet poker.

POT-LIMIT AND NO-LIMIT POKER

Second Edition printed 1999

♠ ♥ ♦ ♣ ♠ ♥ ♦ ♣ ♠ ♥ ♦ ♣ ♠ ♥ ♦ ♣ ♠ ♥ ♦ ♣ ♠ ♥ ♦ ♣ ♠ ♥ ♦ ♣ ♠ ♥ ♦ ♣

DEDICATION

Bob and Stewart rejoice in the many friends they have made through the years playing their favorite poker game of pot-limit Omaha, and the other forms of big-bet poker. We would like to dedicate our book to five players who have helped us and made life more pleasant through the years: Frank Thompson, Donnacha O'Dea, Christer Bjorin, Bob Walker, and Daniel Harrington.

BOOK COVER

We thank Barry Ziderman for doing the cover to our book.

TABLE OF CONTENTS

III - SPECIAL SITUATIONS

IV-GENERAL INFORMATION

V-THE ODDS

1-WHY PLAY POT-LIMIT?
by Bob Ciaffone

Should a player who has played only limit poker try to learn pot-limit play? Nearly all of the world's great poker players would answer this question with a firm and enthusiastic "Yes." What is the magnetic attraction of pot-limit for so many players, especially the good ones?

A pot-size bet offers the would-be caller only 2-1 odds. This contrasts with limit play, where pot odds of 5-1, 10-1, and even 20-1 are commonplace. At limit poker, these favorable odds mean most bets are called, and most pots are won by showing the best hand at the end. A bet or raise at pot-limit confronts the opposition with a far more weighty decision.

Let us look at a typical pot, and contrast limit poker with pot-limit poker. Suppose in a hold'em game there is a $100 pot after the flop. At limit poker, a pot that size is likely the result of playing $10-$20 limit. There is not much leverage in a $10 bet when there is a C-note in the pot. A player does not need to be a good mathematician to make a moderately satisfactory decision. If he thinks there is a chance to win, he plays; otherwise he folds. Drawing to an inside straight is probably a mistake, but not horribly so. Drawing to longshots all evening will eventually take its toll on your finances. But on a single given occasion such as this, it is only a minor peck on one's bankroll.

At pot-limit, in contesting a $100 pot, nearly all bets are in the $50-$100 range. Suppose the opponent bets the limit, as he often does. What should we do? Now drawing to a low-percentage hand like an inside straight will normally be a horrible play. The decision whether to play or fold takes on much more weight. A bad decision will be expensive.

The two forms of poker contrast even more sharply when you start figuring out how much it will cost to play a hand through to the end. At $10-$20 limit poker, a $10 bet after the flop, a $20 bet on fourth street, and a $20 bet on the end comes to a total of $50 to call a betting opponent all the way. At pot-limit, your opponent can bet $100 after the flop. With a $100 pot, a $100 bet, and a $100 call, he will be able to bet $300 on fourth street. The bet on the end could be $900. This is a grand total of $1,300 to see the hand through to the end.

As you can imagine, the bluff is a formidable weapon at pot-limit. The target of a bet has to think about more than just the amount of the bet itself. He also must consider the possibility of being faced with subsequent bets. At pot-limit, not only are the bets far larger in relation to the pot; the subsequent bet size increases at a speedy rate. (A raise skyrockets the pot size even faster.) So a medium-size bet also carries with it a threat to the opponent's entire stack of chips.

Because of the massive leverage attached to a bet or raise at pot-limit poker, the skillful player has a tool to work with that can win a lot of money. At limit poker, you usually win a pot by having the best hand. The virtue of patience in waiting for good hands far outweighs the other poker skills.

We pot-limit players think that poker should not be mainly a contest of patience. We like the far greater role in our game played by skills such as knowing when to bluff, reading our opponent correctly, having the nerve to push a freightload of chips in the pot when the occasion demands it, and knowing the proper odds.

The good players love pot-limit poker because they can use their skills to the fullest extent. Limit poker is a fight between combatants who have to wear handcuffs; pot-limit poker is open warfare. If you are six-and-a-half feet tall and weigh 270 pounds, wouldn't you rather play tackle football instead of touch?

Anyone who has played poker knows the frustration at limit play of trying in vain to make a good hand stand up. Those high pot odds when you bet the best hand mean you are chased by players drawing to inside straights, backdoor flushes, an overcard, a small pair hoping to improve, and a host of other shaky hands. If you could only bet more in relation to the pot size, you could make those chasers let go, or punish them severely for not doing so. Pot-limit play is the cure. No longer do you need to fend off the vultures by wildly flapping your hands; you have a rifle to use.

Obviously, a person who becomes skillful at pot-limit play has the opportunity to make money—a lot of money. Once you become good at poker, it is only logical that you will prefer the form of poker that gives the maximum opportunity to use that talent. That form is clearly pot-limit.

Pot-limit poker does not need to be looked at only with cold monetary eyes. Even though we like to win, we like to have fun doing it. Because of the strong psychological aspect of pot-limit poker, with its clever bluffs, intricately deceptive plays, and emphasis on reading the other fellow's hand, it is a much more enjoyable activity. It is **fun** to bet a few grand at somebody, know by their squirm that you have caught them with the hoped-for hand, and watch them fold a winner. Hauling in a big pot won by a bluff is immensely enjoyable, and gives one the satisfying feeling that the money has been earned, instead of merely being lucky. So, by taking up pot-limit poker, you can fatten your bankroll, and have fun doing it. What more could a person ask for?

2-COMPARING POT-LIMIT TO LIMIT
by Bob Ciaffone

The term pot-limit means just what it says; the limit you can bet is the size of the pot. Naturally, a pot grows in size as a deal progresses, so the betting limit after all the cards are out is usually far greater than it was at the start of that deal.

In some places, the only form of poker played is pot-limit. This is true of Stewart's home country Britain, as well as most other European countries. I remember talking to one of Britain's finest professional poker players, who was coming to America for the first time. The player started asking me for advice on how to play limit poker, saying he had never played that form before!

Americans almost always learn to play limit poker before pot-limit poker. Frankly, this is the natural order, since pot-limit play is more complex. You must decide how much to bet, as well as whether to bet, and decisions are more meaningful, because the amount of a bet or raise is much larger in proportion to the total amount in the pot. Therefore, it will be helpful for many readers if we compare limit and pot-limit betting structures as to their effect on overall strategy.

At limit poker, most bets offer the prospective caller pot odds of anywhere from 4-1 to 20-1. When you bet or raise, these attractive odds mean you are a big favorite to get called. At pot-limit poker, a normal bet is between half the pot size and the full amount of the pot. The pot odds offered the opponent will normally be between 2-1 (for a full-pot bet) and 3-1 (for a half-pot bet). This means at pot-limit a bet or raise has a far better chance of winning immediately, which of course has profound effects on strategy.

If there is a good chance to win the pot with a bet or raise, it is obvious that bluffing becomes much more attractive. To be a good pot-limit player, you must be willing to run bluffs, and become adept at reading your opponents. This means pot-limit is more of a "people game," where psychology is very important.

Pot-limit also puts a high premium on aggressive play. There are two ways to win a pot. You can either show down the best hand at the end, or win earlier by a bet or raise. The difference between being a winning player and a losing player at pot-limit is often determined by how many pots you win without having the best hand. By reaching out with those bets and raises, you win more pots with moderate hands, and also get more action on good hands.

Another difference between pot-limit and limit poker is the use of deception. The good old-fashioned poker virtues of trickery, subterfuge, and chicanery find far more use at pot-limit play. You are constantly scheming how to win all the opponent's chips. Falsely acting weak at some point during the deal can be the way to do it. Another way is to sometimes play a hand that does not measure up to the usual requirements for that situation. The deeper the money, the more reasonable it is to play a surprise holding to bushwhack the opponent with later. And bluffing is of course a form of deception. At limit poker, solid straightforward play is demanded most of the time. At pot-limit, it is often necessary to trick the opponent out of his money. Naturally, this also makes for more fun.

A major difference between the two poker forms is position assumes far more importance at pot-limit. The amount proportionately at risk on each bet makes your decision more meaningful, so giving and getting information for that decision correspondingly increases in value. Acting first is uncomfortable. If you check, a bet by the opponent thus induced can easily knock you out of the pot. If you bet, this alerts the opponent to get out if he does not have a good hand. Acting last is helpful with any hand, but it is especially helpful with marginal hands, because you can act accordingly on the information gained from the opponent. At all forms of poker played with pot-limit betting, the rule for deciding which hands to play is "solid in front, looser in the back."

At limit play, winning with a super-class hand increases the amount you have won by several extra bets, but one bet is only a fraction of the pot size. At big-bet poker, just "one extra bet" actually triples the size of the pot, so a super-class hand earns proportionally a much greater reward. This difference in the amount of reward has a major influence on the relative value of starting hands. For example, at pot-limit or no-limit hold'em, pocket nines are a more desirable starting hand than they are at limit hold'em, and a K-Q offsuit less desirable. Pocket nines build middle set, and K-Q builds only top pair. True, it is more than twice as hard to get a set. But middle set can easily double through an opponent, whereas if top pair breaks someone, it rates to be you. So in building hands at big-bet poker, you take aim at the other person's entire stack.

To sum up, we see that pot-limit poker places much more emphasis on psychology, aggressiveness, deception, and position. The good player thus has more tools to work with. His advantage against weak opponents becomes greater. If your main poker skill is sitting back and waiting for a good hand, you better stay with limit poker. But if you have the finer poker skills—or are willing to work at acquiring them—then pot-limit play is the field where you can really flower.

3-POKER'S TEN COMMANDMENTS
by Stewart and Bob

To win money at big-bet poker—or any other kind of card game—you must be a wise gambler as well as a skilled player. This chapter is concerned with aiding you in that respect. Following these precepts will not necessarily make you into a winning poker player. However, they will make certain that players' eyes don't glisten and their mouths water when you enter the poker room.

(1) NEVER PLAY WITH MONEY YOU CAN'T AFFORD TO LOSE

At pot-limit, everything you have on the table is in play and may all be lost on one hand. Playing with the idea in mind that you will only put a portion of your funds into the pot, unless you have a cinch, is wholly impractical. In poker, most money is made on hands where it is perfectly possible you will wind up losing. The horrible handicap incurred by being unwilling to follow through on good hands far outweighs any technical advantage you may have over your opponents.

A player in a no-limit hold'em game had a fantastic lucky streak. When the game started he had been in desperate financial straits. First he won enough to pay the rent, then to pay back the money he owed left, right and center. At his high water mark, his whole life had turned around. His wife could even be treated to a new dress.

At this point he picked up two aces. The betting before the flop before it even got to him was very fierce. There was a bet and three raises. The correct poker move was to commit all his money. He pondered and dwelt, but the threat of financial ruin was too strong. He mucked the aces and quit the game. Clearly he should have gone home earlier.

(2) ALWAYS KNOW THE RULES OF THE GAME

This seems so obvious, but we've all fallen into the trap. Stewart was once playing in a draw game. He made four of a kind, bet out and everybody passed. He threw away his hand sight-unseen. In conversation a bit later, he mentioned his monster hand. "Oh, you should have shown that," was the comment. "We pay honors for four of a kind or a straight flush." Every poker cardroom has special house rules; learn them.

(3) DON'T STEAM

Playing unsoundly to increase the money fluctuation when you're losing is called steaming. It is the number one vice in the gambling world. The game of poker lends itself well to steaming, because if you are willing to take a bit the worst of it, a player is able to substantially increase the stakes. This is particularly true of no-limit and pot-limit play.

A typical steamer tries to get bigger pots by early raises. Since he does this on hands too weak for such betting, his next step is to try and run opponents out of the pot with bluffs and semi-bluffs. If he manages to catch some hands while doing this, he can turn a losing session into a winning one. More often, the net result of this unsound play will be to go from the frying pan into the fire.

Every successful gambler must first acquire good self-control. Learn to keep score by the week, month or year, instead of trying to put your head on the pillow a winner every night. Nobody wins every session. There is a lot of money to be won from steamers in a no-limit or pot-limit poker games. You cannot let yourself sink to the level of the wild players you are trying to beat. Stay cool and grow rich.

(4) NEVER PLAY WHEN OFF-BALANCE

If you're upset, feeling ill or have a presentiment that you are going to lose, just don't play. There'll always be another game.

One of the most ridiculous errors we encounter is where a

player has a marvelous hand but fails to raise and capitalize on his good fortune. When asked why, the reply is, "I've been doing so badly I didn't want to take the risk." Of course, and his bad run will continue.

The big pot factor means the possibility of cheating, whether real or imagined, is more dangerous than in limit. An Omaha player returned to his seat from a phone call to find a hand containing two aces. The flop came A-10-10, giving him aces full. To his amazement, there was bet and a raise before he acted. After reflection, he mucked his hand, fearing a set-up. One player won the pot with A-10, beating the other who held the case 10 and filled up. If the aces full player hadn't been so paranoid, he would have tripled his money. Don't play in games where you feel uncomfortable. You want neither to be cheated, nor to play a hand abnormally for fear there has been some monkey business.

(5) RUN YOUR PROFITS AND CUT YOUR LOSSES

We learnt this one from the stock market. At poker, when you are winning, you feel better, play better and the opponents fear you. This last factor is of paramount importance at pot-limit, where intimidation plays such a giant role.

Nobody plays as well when losing as when winning. It is not a bad idea to sit out a few hands after losing a major pot. Losing shouldn't upset your equanimity. But eventually it will, and once it does, obey Commandment Four and quit.

(6) DON'T BE A CALLING STATION

There are players who seldom bet or raise; they just call. This is a recipe for total disaster. There is nothing wrong with calling and then lashing out with a raise later in the hand. But you need to make a play for the pot at some point. Being able to bet or raise the size of the pot means there is a far better chance of winning it immediately than at limit play. You must exploit this factor.

(7) DON'T GIVE OR RECEIVE AGGRAVATION

There is no percentage in deliberately trying to upset your opponents by your comments or actions. For one thing, people should enjoy playing poker. We pity you if your kicks come from spoiling other people's pleasure. Strong players won't react to being needled. Weak ones will simply give up playing with you. Proper behavior, besides having intrinsic merit, may gain you access to many favorable gaming situations out of reach for irritating personalities.

The term "aggro" was coined in England especially for this concept. Of course, you should never allow yourself to become annoyed. That's just a variation on the Third Commandment.

(8) DON'T GET TRICKY AGAINST A WEAK PLAYER

We have often seen so-called experts make a sophisticated bluffing play. The weakie calls, explaining apologetically, "I knew you had the flush, but I had to call with my two pair." Here there is no difference from limit poker. Complexity can only succeed against good players.

(9) DON'T GET INVOLVED WHERE YOU ARE EITHER A SMALL FAVORITE OR A BIG DOG

This is the mostly clearly exemplified in hold'em. You hold 6-6 before the flop and the second raise comes to you. This will be either from a hand such as A-K or a high pair. You are perhaps 11/10 favorite against any non-pair, but more than a 4-1 underdog against a larger pair. At limit poker this presents no problems. At pot-limit, pass this hand. It can only lead to grief over time.

The principle can be extended well beyond poker. The Lloyd's of London names are the final underwriters of insurance policies. Their profits come from the premiums paid to insure against risks. Their losses arise when disaster strikes. The liability is unlimited and their profit a set sum. Everything went well for 300 years, and the "players" sat back and made their profits with virtually no work. Then an unusual number of high claims in succession bankrupted some very rich people.

Selling short in the stock market suffers from the same problem. The price of a stock cannot sink below zero, but it can rise to undefined heights. If you can't get out in time, sooner or later you are going to go bankrupt.

(10) DON'T PLAY IN A GAME UNLESS YOU FIGURE TO WIN

Being a decent player does not ensure an edge. You could be the tenth best player in the world, but if you sit down in the game with the nine people who are better than you, they figure to get your money. The attractiveness of a game is determined primarily by the number of weak players in it. Without a couple of soft spots, you're likely to be better off watching TV.

Another major factor affecting your edge is the rake-off. Some places take so much out of the pot, the only winner at the end of the year is the house. A pot-limit player must be especially beware of any game raked on a straight percentage basis with no ceiling. Although the average pot may be no bigger than that in a comparable limit game, the biggest pots will be much larger. Don't let a big rake rob you.

(11) VARY YOUR PLAY

Unlike the original Ten Commandments, ours do not come from a Higher Power, and are thus not cut in stone. So we present an eleventh commandment. Vary your play, even if this means you must occasionally break one of the other ten in order to do so. This assumes special importance when playing regularly with the same group of people.

Several Las Vegas players tell the story of arriving in town with a few hundred dollars to their name and an old car to sleep in. They couldn't afford to play poker at all, but they did anyway. They had no good alternative route to a prosperous life, and here they are, alive and kicking, over a quarter-century later.

You may have a cold, but the game is so good you simply must continue. It's clear all the easy money may have dried up before your cold has run its course.

Sometimes one player is an inveterate bettor. But, as soon as you bet or raise in a particular hand, he switches off. Now, most unusually, passive play is best.

A game could be so attractive, although you don't want to risk more capital, you are prepared to gamble what you have left in front of you. If that's your bag, then occasionally go for it.

Yes, the rules are all there waiting to be broken. But usually let the other players be the ones to incur the wrath of the poker gods.

4-YOUR PLAYING STYLE
by Bob Ciaffone

There is no one mold that has casted successful big-bet poker players, or even World Champions. There is considerable variance as to the number of starting hands played, aggressiveness, table image, and a host of other characteristics. My collaborator Mr. Reuben plays more attacking poker and has a fiercer table image than I do. But we both get the job done. It is up to each individual player to develop a style of plays that best suits him. Were I to try and mimic Stew's style, it is likely that my results would suffer, and perhaps vice-versa.

But in all honesty, I feel that the solid style of play that I use is the best approach for the majority of players. If you play a lot of hands and are constantly using money to fight your way out of tight spots, you better be excellent at reading situations and opponents. Simply put, you need the highest quality of poker skills to be successful with a very aggressive style of play. And there will be wider fluctuations in your bankroll.

Note that having a generally solid approach doesn't mean you totally abandon such risky plays as raising a hold'em pot on a 7-6 suited, and so forth. You shouldn't be completely predictable. It is only the frequency of such a play that distinguishes the solid player from the very aggressive player.

Most aggressive players are not in high gear all the time. A good aggressive player is tuned into the situation and knows how much he can get away with. If the game is so weak that nearly all his bets are getting called, he is going to back off and start showing down winners.

Please note that this difference in playing style primarily takes place early in the deal. We are talking about such things as how many hands to play and how often to raise the pot. Later on when you have a substantial amount of information about the enemy holding, it becomes less a question of style. There is likely a right and wrong thing to do by that time, and any good player is supposed to do the right thing. If that "right thing" calls for a bold bluff, even a solid player like myself is going to put the money into the pot.

I think it is a mistake to sit down at the table and say to yourself, "I am going to play super-solid tonight." Or, "I am going to do some gambling this evening." We do not know what cards are going to be dealt to us. If we start out with a nice run of hands, we will look like we are doing a lot of gambling, though we may actually have a good hand each time we have bet or raised. And if we hold the usual collection of ugliness, it will look as if we are playing tight poker, even though to play any of the terrible hands we have been dealt might make us a candidate for a mental institution. So do not decide ahead of time how to play, so much as go with the flow of the cards, and base your actions on how the other players are perceiving you at that point in the session.

5-HOW DEEP ARE YOU?
by Bob Ciaffone

The amount of money in front of the players has a profound influence on the betting. The deeper the money, the greater the implication that a player has a strong hand when he raises. His raise also exerts greater leverage, because the amount that may be put at risk in further betting must be considered. Naturally, this intensifies the psychological aspects of the situation as well. Position greatly increases in importance with large stacks of chips. It would be improper to construct a big-bet poker problem and not state how much money was in front of each player.

Let us look at a no-limit hold'em game and see how the amount of money in front of us and our opponent affects our decision when we raise a pot and get reraised. Assume the game has a $25 minimum bring-in, we open for $100, and get repopped.

(1) We and the opponent both started with $200, so the reraise is $100 more all-in. This is the easiest situation in poker. We don't bother to look at our hand, or analyze what the opponent might have. We just put the money in and see who wins. You are too deeply involved to fold.

(2) We and the opponent both started with $350, so the raise is $250 more all-in. Here the raise is about the size of the pot. If I were trying to steal with a Q-J (suited or not) my inclination would be to fold. On any legitimate raising hand, such as an A-Q suited or a pair of 10's, I would call.

(3) We and the opponent both started with $600, so the raise is $500 more all-in. The fact that my opponent overbet the pot size to move in is not of all that great consequence as to what he holds. In fact, had he only raised us $200 more rather than going all-in, it might well be a more dangerous situation. In the latter case, it would look as if he were treading lightly to induce a call. Of course, a lot depends on who the opponent is in deducing what sort of psychology he might be using. In the actual problem, even though the opponent might well not have a big pair, we are not so committed to the pot. It is time to start

looking carefully at what we hold, who raised us, the psychology involved, and other such factors. My inclination would be to require a solid hand such as A-K or J-J to call.

(4) We both start the hand with a grand; the opponent raises my $100 bet $250 more, so he has another $650 left. Beware! This differs night and day from the situation where we were raised $250 more all-in. In the present circumstance, the opponent is very likely to hold a big hand. There is no hand that I would call him with. My only choices are to either fold or raise. I would be too far into the pot to be throwing my hand away for the bet on the flop, because the last $650 would be equal to or less than the pot size if I call his raise. To play for all my money, I would almost surely have either aces or kings (which are the likely hands for my opponent to hold).

(5) We both start the hand with three thousand dollars. The opponent reraises my $100 raise $250 more, so there is now $2,650 left—enough for two more raises. Strangely, there is actually a greater chance that your opponent is fooling around here than in the previous situation. He is risking a much lower percentage of his stack, and the intimidation factor is even greater. Nevertheless, it is foolish to reraise him on kings or queens here. There is only one hand that is a through ticket for all your money; aces. Look at the situation this way: If you reraise with kings, how could your opponent possibly make a mistake? He will go all-in with aces, and fold everything else. It is better to call with kings, and try to make some money with them if they're good. To reraise, you need aces—or a bluff.

Now that we have talked about how the size of your stack affects heads-up play, lets talk about multihanded situations. Suppose in a hold'em game player A opens for a raise to $100, and player B raises $250 more, making the total bet $350 to you. To fully understand the situation, you need to know how much money is in front of each opponent. For example, suppose player A had $350, and player B $1,000. It is quite possible that player B only had in mind taking a race against player A for $350, and is not prepared to play for his whole stack. The situation would be quite different if player A also had a grand. Whether your own stack is

$200, $500, or $1,000, it is still necessary to consider how much player B thought he was going to be playing for when he reraised.

Akin to this idea is the situation where you have raised the pot and have many callers. Suppose you have two aces, and after the flop hits, the first player leads through you with a medium-sized bet. Even though you think those aces are still the best hand, it would be dangerous, and probably incorrect, for you to raise with the whole field yet to be heard from. Beware of bushwhackers. This is especially important when you have a lot of money, the bettor or raiser only has a small stack, but someone else with a live hand is deep in dough.

Should you lead right out with a big hand, or look for a check-raise? A major factor affecting your decision is the depth of the money. Suppose at hold'em you are heads-up against a raiser, and fortunately flop a set of trips. What is the best way to nail him for his whole stack? Let us assume there is $250 in the pot. We will look at three situations:

(I) You each have $250 left. It is almost surely right to check and hope the opponent moves all-in. If he also checks, he will wonder whether a future bet by you shows a good hand or simply has assumed weakness on his part because he checked.

(II) You each have $1,000 left. Here it is still probably better to check, intending to raise him all-in if he bets. (Checking and calling, a broken wing act, is also a consideration.) Note that if he bets the size of the pot, a raise the size of the pot will put you all-in. In this sequence the opponent does not know if you have a big hand or are simply willing to go all-in with a moderate hand.

(III) You each have $3,000 left. Here a check-raise clearly shows the ability to play for big money, and enables the opponent to get away from his hand cheaply. A better chance to double up is usually to lead out into the opponent. This works especially well when there is a potential draw available such as a two-flush on the board. A lot of players will raise you here if they hold a big pair. This gets them so deeply I involved that they may well go for it when you move in on them. Leading right out with a topnotch hand is often the better play when the money is very deep. This also helps protect you against the opponent picking off a miracle card such as a gutshot straight, which is hard on both your bankroll and your equanimity.

As we see, the amount of money in front of you and your opponent is often a critical factor in determining whether to play and how to play. This is a major difference between limit poker and big-bet poker. It is the reason why a player is entitled to ask, "How deep are you?" before he acts on his hand.

ADDENDUM BY STEWART

The depth of the money also determines your strategy when you have a drawing hand. Often the direct odds you are offered are inadequate, but the implied odds give you a reason to call. For other aspects, see the chapter "Probability Concepts."

This is easiest to understand in hold'em. You hold 7♠–6♠. Perhaps you have stuck your neck out and raised. Anyway, a player has raised and you are certain he has a reasonable hand. You are the only two players in the pot. Should you call?

Clearly, if the raise is all-in, then 2 to 1 for your money is inadequate. The general rule of thumb that professionals seem to use for such a call is you want the potential to win about twenty times the current bet you are facing. Of course, it won't help if you are facing a $100 bet and have $2000 yourself, but the adversary has short money. Your opponent must be playing on at least $2000.

This should give you an idea why some people like to conceal how deep they are. If they can obscure the facts, you may make the incorrect strategic decision. Thus, these players like to play with bills rather than chips. Only chips play in London for this reason. Even then, sometimes players may hide their large chips. Naturally, you don't want to show too much interest in how deep your opponent is, as that could be giving away too much information.

The reason you need to be able to win so much in hold'em is because it is so difficult to hit your hand. Matters are quite different in Omaha. Consider a hand like 9-8-6-5 unsuited. You can certainly call a bet from aces double-suited with equanimity. The hand you most fear is 9-8-6-5 double-suited, which gives the opponent a total freeroll. And a hand such as 10-9-8-7 could put you in bad shape on a lot of flops.

Seven-card stud is different again. Holding 8-7-3 suited with live cards against a raiser is an easy call at limit. At pot-limit with only you and the raiser left it should normally be discarded. If you make your four-flush next card, you may still have to face a series of large bets. On each of your next two upcards, the opponent can see whether you have made a possible flush, and act accordingly. He can fold when you catch a three-flush on board and bet the size of the pot when you do not. However deep you are, the money is still likely to run out before you make your hand if you keep calling. Note that if the opponent bets the size of the pot with only one more card to come, you will be getting such a bad price on your flush-draw that it would be better to fold at that point.

Lowball and high-low variations depend more on the probability you are winning than the value of the implied odds of the out-draw.

Now it should be easy to see why if you are playing with low funds, you must play tighter than if you cover the table. If you play with very substantial funds, then you may play looser still. A few small errors can be compensated by that one big win in a later pot. Also, when you are drawing, there will be ammunition to fire if you hit—or wish to bluff.

6-HOW MUCH TO BET
by Stewart Reuben

In pot-limit there is little to be said for betting the pot to the nearest dollar. For example, if the pot stands at $110, then $100 is more sensible than squeezing out the last drop of blood. In the middle of the hand this slows down the action, because everybody calling will require change. Within this parameter, there remains considerable sense in betting or raising the whole pot. Then it is easy to keep track of its size. A pot is $1200, and a player before you bets $1200; it is easy to know the raise is up to $3600. Thus, for a dealer or player, knowledge of the three-times-table is an asset. With two people in the pot prior to your action, it is the four-times-table.

It is extremely useful to carry the precise size of the pot in your head at all times for two quite different reasons. I have played in games where certain dealers might palm a chip. By announcing the size of the pot, I have been able to inhibit this action. No matter that it wasn't my money I was saving directly. Any money remaining with the players is potentially mine. The other reason is that it enables you to bet a sum other than the pot for reasons which are then unclear to the opposition.

If you have a monster of a hand, you may want to offer apparently good odds to your opponents. If you are putting through a bluff, betting less than the pot means you are giving yourself better than even money. If you play with me, you'll find I often bet less than the whole pot. It is impossible to tell whether I am strong or weak from this.

Sometimes it is you to act and you don't know whether or not you have the best hand. Now it makes sense to bet considerably less than the pot because you don't want to give a free card to a drawing hand. Unfortunately, if this ploy is obvious, your opponent can pick up on it and raise as a good bluff.

Other times you may be so strong you don't want to bet the pot because your opponent is much worse than a 2-1 underdog.

Again, your opponent could realize this and pass a hand he would have called if you had bet the whole pot.

Sometimes you have what looks like a monster, but in fact is rather weak. For example, at seven-card stud, holding (3C 7H) 7S 9S AS 10S, facing a board which is nothing much. A bet offering 3-1 now looks like you are crying out to be called. If he does call, bet an even smaller fraction of the pot on the river. Now a good player may well reckon you really do have the flush. If he does call, well, it was relatively inexpensive. Remember, don't get fancy with a weakie!

Similarly, in Omaha on fifth street, with the board showing 7C JD 8H 9D 4D, your opponent bets out on the end. Now with the bare ace of diamonds, you may have a better chance of securing a pass with a small raise than a large one.

In Omaha particularly, it sometimes pays to give an opponent better odds than he thinks he needs because you have more information. For example, you hold Q-J-8-8 ; the flop is 10-9-2. An opponent bets and you call. The pot is now two-handed and stands at $1000. On fourth street, the board is (10-9-2)-8 with no open two-flush. Your opponent checks. If he has 10-10-?-? then he thinks he is 3.2 to 1 against filling up. You know he has only 7 outs, so that he is 5-1. What is more, the case eight will devastate him. Bet $350. This offers him 4-1 from where he stands. You may lose the pot, but you must take risks in order to win big. It is no different from checking the nut flush on the flop. A strong player may guess what you are up to, but he is powerless.

This being Omaha, he may have K-Q-10-10, and you are giving him the odds he needs. What is more, you may find it hard to pass a bet if a jack pops up. For this reason, you are much more in danger holding 9-8-7-7 with a board of J-10-2-7. This needs a pot bet because there are so many potentially larger straights to destroy your hand. In fact, the whole situation is so ugly, your hand should have been mucked on the flop. You had 12 straightening cards, but only two of them were the nuts. In our first example you had 16 straight cards, of which 10 were the stone-cold nuts.

In half-pot you are much more likely to want to bet the absolute maximum in order to squeeze the last drop of advantage from the pot. At Omaha you hold the straight. You are virtually certain he has trips and you have no defense. It is essential to bet the maximum because, having done so, he is now receiving 3-1 for his money and is only 3.2 to 1 against. Also, he must call, as there is some chance you are bluffing.

Where there are three or more players in the pot and one has a fairly short stack, there are opportunities for some fancy plays. But you must be fast and accurate. It is no good asking how much the player has left; you are going to have to take your action apparently innocently. For this reason it is better if only chips are used; then it is easier to count an opponent down. For example, suppose there is $5K in the pot. You are first to speak with unlimited funds (what a dream), Sid follows with unlimited funds, and Dave is last to speak holding $8K. If you are very strong, you should bet more than $4K. This way Sid knows that if Dave raises all-in, you will not be able to reraise. He is thus more likely to call. If you are weak, then the better play is less than $4K. Now Sid may pass, knowing he may have to face two raises. Consider London lowball. Dave follows you. Currently you are winning but would dearly like Sid to stack. The correct play is to bet $2K into the $5K pot. Dave raises $6K. Now Sid must call $8K to win $15K. You have shaded his odds down below 2-1, whereas a pot bet would have given him 21-8. Moreover, you threaten a reraise of $29K, so that he is then risking a fortune. He is likely to back off. Dave may not cooperate and pass or just call. That isn't so terrible. Sid has been given a cheap ticket to seventh street, but the pot is smaller, and there is less to worry about. It may seem a check would have done the job even better, but you want Sid out, and a check-raise always gives him 2-1.

Naturally now you know this, provided the opposition has also read this book, you can use reverse psychology in these coups and play the hand the other way round. That is why I put so much emphasis on knowing the precise pot size, disguising your knowledge, and knowing how deep the money is. Then it is impossible for the enemy to know your motive for betting that precise sum of money. Keep them guessing and off-balance.

You can see from the preceding discussion the dreadful effect on play when the dealer announces the pot size, either because of a foolish house policy that he do so, or by simply volunteering information that was not asked. Both your bets and those of an opponent take on a different meaning when it is obvious that both of you are aware of exactly how much is in the pot. For this reason (and others) we big-bet players much prefer the dealer remain silent unless the player makes a direct inquiry about the pot size. For more on this see our chapter, "Dealing Big-bet Poker."

Where there are still several players to act, the chance of running a bluff successfully diminishes sharply. Also, having bet, as each opponent calls, the odds are improved for the next player. This is a little understood double-edged factor. If there is a pot bet and four players have called in front of you, then you have meaty odds of 6-1. But you have to fight five other players for the pot. Your probability of winning goes down. Clearly, in flop games, where, if you make your hand it is less likely the opposition can win, the more the merrier. In stud or draw games, you may indeed make your hand, but be devastated by one of the other players.

7-TAKING THE INITIATIVE
by Bob Ciaffone

The initiative is important at any form of poker. At big-bet poker, this importance is magnified even more so. When you can bet enough in proportion to the pot that many types of hands are forced to fold, a bet or raise becomes a more powerful play. Aggressiveness will win a lot of pots without much of a fight.

There is another aspect of the initiative that is extremely important at pot-limit and no-limit play. Someone who bets or raises is taking the most aggressive action possible at that point. Therefore, he has an unlimited hand. There is a chance he holds the mortal nuts. The player who checks or calls has a limited hand, at least in theory. (Naturally, a player can turn up with the nuts on some mighty peculiar betting sequences.) This has a profound effect on subsequent betting.

Let's look at a couple of typical poker situations, and see when having the initiative is quite valuable.

(1) At Omaha high, you pick up a hand that includes a pair of queens. The flop comes to your liking; Q♠-9♣-4♠. You lead at the pot with your top set and get one caller. The fourth street card is the J♣, making a possible straight, and also creating the possibility of a backdoor flush on the last card. Even if you're one of the world's great poker players, there's scarcely any way to know at this point whether that jack made the opponent a straight. If you bet, the opponent does not really know whether you have made straight with that jack, or are still betting with whatever caused you to bet the flop. But if you check, you are now on the defensive. The opponent can take a free card. If he bets, you have too much hand to fold and not enough hand to raise. Your check and subsequent call pinpoint your values quite closely. He will put you on a hand such as top two pair or a set. He also knows you are most unlikely to have picked up a club draw. If you had enough hand to bet the flop and picked up a flush-draw on fourth street, why would you check? Are

you Casper Milquetoast? As you can see, a check limits your hand and puts the opponent in the driver's seat. He may even charge you a price to hit a full on fourth street, and run a big bluff on the end if non-threatening card hits. If you check and call on fourth street, a bet of this type on the end will be hard to call.

(2) At hold'em, the flop comes 9-4-4 of three different suits. You bet, and get one caller. Has your opponent limited his hand by failing to raise? Not really. A free card is most unlikely to let you draw out if he has an extremely powerful hand such as pocket nines or pocket fours. In fact, it would actually be more normal for somebody with this strong a hand to smooth-call rather than raise. The raise may let the cat out of the bag too soon. As you see, the principle of the bettor or raiser having an unlimited hand and the caller having a limited hand does not apply here. The principle applies only when the texture of the board makes it dangerous to give a free or cheap card.

We can conclude that the initiative is of limited value when the nuts can afford to leave the opponent in the pot because there is little danger of being outdrawn. In the hold'em layout given, knowing nothing about the opposing hands or players, you would not know whether to make a side bet on the bettor or the caller. Actually, the caller is more likely to show up with a real hand. But in the Omaha example, with a layout that will let the next boardcard create a "new nuts" much of the time, a player who fails to take aggressive action has conveyed immense information about his hand. (Of course, there is no law against someone making a deceptive play, but there is a lot of risk attendant to giving a free or cheap card here.) These two situations we discussed are at opposite ends of the spectrum, and naturally there is plenty of middle ground between them, but you can see the principle that is involved.

You will find in big-bet poker that it is extremely important for the opponent to fear that you might have the nuts. By having the initiative in situations where your hand is unlimited, you can pick up a lot of pots, and keep would-be bullies from pushing you around. If you dog it, the opponent may take the initiative—and the pot—away from you.

The preceding discussion has focused on the value of having an unlimited hand. At big-bet poker, there is another reason for you to bet or raise. The pot increases in size many times over what the normal growth pattern would be in a limit poker game, and the wager size increases in corresponding fashion. If you have a powerful hand and unnecessarily allow an opponent to draw out on you, the penalty is severe.

Let's use an example from hold'em. Suppose the flop comes K-8-2, and you have 8-8, giving you middle set. Assume that there is 1K in the pot, and both you and the opponent have 10K stacks. If you give a free card on the flop and an opponent picks off a 9 on fourth street holding that pair in the pocket, it is going to cost you at least 4K, and probably all ten grand. Compare this with limit poker, where the penalty besides losing the grand in the pot figures to be less than an additional 1K. A big-bet poker player has to be alert to the possibility of a huge adverse swing by giving a free card. Note that if your hand had been **top** set, it would have been your opponent who was taking the nose-dive from hitting that nine. A good idea is to ask yourself this question: "If I give a free card, is my opponent going to get rich or go broke as a result of improving?"

8-DRAWING HANDS
by Bob Ciaffone

At big-bet poker, playing a drawing hand such as a four-straight or four-flush involves quite a change in strategy from its counterpart at limit play, because the math and psychology are so different. At limit play, it would be rare to fold a four-straight or four-flush for a single bet, because the pot odds warrant a call. Big-bet poker strategy often says a fold is in order, because a pot-size bet means such a hand is not getting adequate odds to play.

Let's look at a typical pot-limit hold'em situation where you turn a flush-draw. Suppose you hold Q♣-J♣ and the flop comes K♠-8♣-6♣. There is $100 in the pot. Three of you have stayed for the flop. The first player bets $100, the middle player folds, and it is up to you. What action do you take?

Resist the impulse to play. You have a clear fold, for several reasons:

(1) The pot-odds are insufficient. You have 9 cards that make the flush, out of a total number of 47 unknown cards (52 less the 2 in your hand and the 3 on the board). This means you are over a 4-1 underdog to make the flush (only 9 wins, and 38 non-wins). The pot odds are only 2-1. (There is $200 in the pot after your opponent's bet, and it costs you $100 to call). The pot odds dictate a fold.

(2) The implied odds don't help much. If you make the flush, your opponent will see that there are now three clubs on the board. You are not all that likely to extract more money from him on this layout of cards.

(3) You are not hitting to the nuts. This is a key point at big-bet poker. One of the nine cards that makes your flush pairs the board. None of the eight non-pairing flush cards will make you the nuts either. Suppose your opponent is betting on the nut flush-draw or top pair and a flush-draw. Such bets are commonplace. This dreadful situation puts you with the

worse hand going in, and places you in position to take a big loss if you hit what you are hoping for.

There are a lot better drawing hands you could hold than this queen-high flush-draw. Let's talk about them. We'll use this same flop of K♠-8♣-6♣.

(I) 9♥-7♥. Hey, what's this? How could a simple straight-draw be better than a flush-draw? You only have eight cards that make the straight, and two of them (the 10♣ and the 5♣) could make someone a flush. Well, the straight-draw has a couple of things going for it. First, if you hit the hand, you figure to make some money on it, because the opponent will not fear a ten or a five like he fears a club. Second, if a flush card comes, you are well-placed to launch a successful bluff, especially in position.

(II) A♣-2♣. The nut flush-draw may win by pairing the ace, and there is the possibility of catching the opponent on a flush-draw, making the implied odds attractive. If the flush comes, you clean up.

(III) K♣-Q♣ Top pair and a flush-draw. This gives you a hand that may be good, and can draw out if it's not.

(IV) 10♣-9♣ This gives you a gutshot straight-draw to go with the flush-draw. Even though it's only three more outs, this changes the math considerably. Also, the implied odds are in your favor because the straight may well get paid off.

(V) 9♣-7♣. A straight-flush draw is a powerful holding.

We must consider the possibility of raising the pot when we have a good drawing hand. At big-bet poker such a wager gives us a good chance to win the pot right there. Which hands are the more suitable for raising?

I am much more likely to prefer a raise to a call when I have a good drawing hand, but am **not** hitting to the nuts. When my non-nut draw is a pair and flush-draw or a straight-draw and flush-draw, I can never be sure the flush is good when it comes. My tendency is to whack the opponent with a big raise and hope he folds. If he goes with me, I know that my hand has plenty of outs, even though I'm not sure what they are.

When you gun it out on the flop with a draw, you get to look at two cards without having to pay again for the second card. This of course changes the odds considerably. With a big draw, you may even become the favorite.

The situation you want to avoid with a draw is to get a lot of money committed to the pot—perhaps from a quarter to half your stack—and be out of position with one card to come. The opponent, who may have a good idea what you have by this time, will attempt to bail out if you hit and set you all-in if you miss.

To avoid this unpleasant situation, we must go back to the beginning of the hand and cure the root of the problem. If you are deep enough in money that a check-raise will leave you out on a limb rather than all-in with no more decisions, then you must avoid building a drawing hand. Up front with deep money, you must play "pair poker" for your starting hands. The top players are strong about avoiding drawing hands up front.

Naturally, it's an imperfect world, and we can never be sure what we're building. But you can make an intelligent guess and play the percentages. If you are a hold'em player and pick up a J-10 suited or an 8-7 suited, it is more likely that you will flop a draw rather than a made hand. Muck those hands up front, especially when the money is deep. You can also see that a draw is a worse hand up front in pot-limit than in no-limit. At least at no-limit you have a way to not caught out-of-position with half your stack in the pot on fourth street; scoot it all to the middle!

The willingness to play a drawing hand aggressively, even committing all your money on occasion, puts an element of uncertainty in your opponent's mind. "Does he have a big hand, or is he drawing?" You'd be surprised how often a player who is stuck in the game manages to convince himself that your big bet is probably based on a draw. Of course, getting your good made hands paid off is crucial to your bankroll.

When drawing, and trying to figure out whether to call a bet or raise, it is particularly important to figure in the chance of making money after all the cards are out. In other words, you must guess what the implied odds are, as well as thinking about the price on drawing out. If the game uses boardcards, where the opponent can see the card you got, this can either hurt or help your situation. If the cards that improve your hand are the ones that your opponent is going to figure you for, as is usually the case with a flush-draw, this means you are unlikely to get paid off. Also, you will be unable to bluff if you strike out. On the other hand, if you are hitting to a hand that will be a surprise to your opponent, this is a highly favorable aspect, both in making you money when hitting, and letting you bluff successfully when missing. If the last card is concealed, as in stud or draw, the implied odds are always helpful. For a thorough discussion of this type of situation where the card is unknown to your adversary, be sure to read the chapter (following our London Lowball chapter) called "Important Pot-limit Concepts."

9-PSYCHOLOGY
by Stewart Reuben

People who know nothing about poker often assume it to be a game purely of percentages. In truth it is quintessentially a people game. Knowing whether your opponents are pushy, timid, fearless, incapable of passing when they have a glimmer of a chance, soft callers, kind to their opponents, frightened of getting involved, rocks, drunk, tired, emotionally upset, penniless, caked up, on coke, at death's door, or on tilt, counts for much more than knowing you are an 11-10 underdog rather than 6-5. This is why many of the better players are extremely solicitous of the health of their opponents and family. They are being sociable, may have a genuine interest and are trying to create a friendly ambiance for the amateur. Yet, there will still be an underlying measure of self-interest. After all, I need healthy opponents so that they will continue playing poker.

SOCIAL DYNAMICS

To the best of my knowledge nobody has written a serious doctoral thesis on this subject—yet it is utterly fascinating.

One quite commonly plays in a game which is completely drab. Then somebody will mutter to me about how bad the game is. This is usually the player who is the prime cause of the lack of action. Where everybody is only taking up premium hands, it is essential to follow suit to some extent. It is true you can snatch off a number of small pots. The problem is that in each case you find yourself confronted only by the best hand among the other seven players. This is a tough burden to overcome. I remember playing in a four-handed game where for 30 minutes there was no bet at all. The player who had to bring in the forced bet won the antes. Of course we stopped playing. Well, we had never really started.

Then, there is a change of just one person in the game and the whole dynamics of the action alters. Now the game becomes a rip-roaring blockbuster. This is not necessarily because the player is a weak loser. I have frequently had that effect on a game myself. So much so, that when invited to sit in on a game, I have only half-jokingly suggested they pay my table money. It has been mentally disturbing when they have agreed. Similarly a player can have a stultifying effect; as soon as he sits down, the game dies. The players don't want to give the boring rock action.

Equally, once one player starts to play aggressively, trying to snatch off the antes, the others perforce follow suit. That is why it is perfectly feasible to play in one game where you don't even consider calling with a certain hand and in another where you are willing to take the same holding to the river. Thus the flop is A-10-3 in Omaha. In some games, holding 6-5-3-3, I put my head down and charge. In others, a casual flip of the wrist mucks the hand immediately should somebody breathe on the pot.

Some professionals behave appallingly when the star attraction gets up from the table. They straight-away follow suit. Now the star may be a dreadful poker player, but that doesn't make him a fool. Couldn't they show some tact and wait a few minutes? Even the biggest idiot will eventually catch on that he was the only value in the game. If nothing else, it may hurt his ego. You want the inveterate losers to feel at home; otherwise it will hurt your pocketbook.

A businessman was once leaving the poker table in Las Vegas after having thrown off a nice lump of money. Suddenly he turned and said, "You'll probably laugh at me once I'm out of earshot. I come here three or four times a year and blow off some energy and steam. Whenever I return, you are always sitting here, trying to scratch out a living. You tell me, who's the mug?"

I have often wished I could eavesdrop on the comments about myself when away from the game. If nothing else, it would be extremely revealing and thus most profitable. Should I set up a bug? Has anybody ever done so? I am certain players have sat in games with foreigners whose language they understand, but have not let on. The supposedly unintelligible conversations can be most illuminating.

Being a purist, I find those who profess a deep interest in the welfare of their weak opponents distasteful. Gushingly asking how they are and how the family is doing is extremely false. But let's be honest; poker is a game of play-acting. Some opponents do react positively to such an approach. Nobody has ever accused me of being the greatest diplomat in the world. Sometimes a player will feel a moral imperative to go easy on an opponent with whom they have a good social relationship. Personally, I find it more profitable to take no prisoners. But the beauty of poker is that what is right for one player may be totally wrong for another.

Outsiders often mistakenly think the players must be at each other's throats, both on and off the tables. This is by no means necessarily so. Players often have close social relationships with each other. People are often truly distressed when another player has been destroyed by a particularly virulent outdraw. Such a social reaction is less prevalent in a limit game.

Poker games sometimes run continuously for days on end. I am sure it is a big advantage to be clean-living, not staying up for several days, and especially not being on coke or speed.

In England, and frequently in America, a game will start at a fairly set time, and run its natural course for less than a day. Pot-limit games grow in size as the day wears on. This is because the winners are naturally playing with more money. The losers usually like to maintain on the table at least half of the money they are stuck. This way they can get out of it in one shot. If there is a set closing time, often the game becomes wilder at the end, as the losers desperately raise to build big pots. Of course, they are being illogical; tomorrow is another day. Thus such expressions as "lift off" or "entering phase four."

MENTAL CHARACTERISTICS OF OPPONENTS

Although nothing is of greater importance than knowing your own mental framework, there is no doubt that your opponent's way of thinking is of great importance. If you are able to take it further, to how they think you think, now the game is really entering its existential final stage. Unfortunately, you are now also up against high-quality opponents. There is little profit here, and I seek new pastures. If playing in a money game against all the best players in the world is your bag, so be it. I view poker as more of a game of mistakes than forced errors.

If your opponent is pushy, then it often pays simply to lie back and await his attack. This contradicts the generally held view that it is essential to be aggressive. If your opponent is timid, it often pays to underbet the pot so that he will be less likely to pass in fear of losing too much money. Of course, the nature of life is that you will usually not have the best hand, so that blasting him out is the best policy.

It is very useful, when joining a game already in progress, to find out how everybody is doing. I like to play with a large sum of money on the table to disguise my standing. If you can persuade somebody who has been at the table for some time to cough up the information, so much the better. I used to have one friend who would toke me a chip for information on somebody he hadn't previously encountered. On one occasion I told him the player was a complete stranger to me. After the slightest hesitation, he pushed the chip over. Of course, my info still was informative, although perhaps not as much so as telling him the player had only one week to live.

Players react differently when down to their last few chips. Also, you mustn't confuse the situations where somebody is doing badly in a game with that where they have struck rock-bottom in life. Some players will think, "What the hell," and throw in the money out of desperation. Others will become extremely conservative and try to hold on until they have a lock. Generally, people are most reluctant to take tenuous action when they are level after a long session, having bobbed up and down—especially if they have only just gotten back to level. Now, they are most vulnerable to a bluff. They simply do not want to get involved. That is why the correct winning attitude is that life is just one long poker game.

It does help to know when somebody is emotionally disturbed for reasons outside the game. Sometimes this can lead them to play better! Usually we tend to play a sequence of hands aggressively, then perhaps a group more defensively, and so on. Of course, a better strategy is to mix up your play so that the opposition has no clues as to where you are at. Imagine playing after breaking up with a girlfriend. A few hands pass without your thinking about the situation; then it comes to mind and you play like a savage beast. Suddenly you have a mood shift. How can the opposition cope with that? We don't usually have visible emotional indicators on our heads—I hope.

10-READING THE OPPONENT
by Bob Ciaffone

Acquiring the ability to read opponents well is more difficult than gaining mastery over technical skills such as knowledge of probabilities and understanding hand values. You need a lot of on-the-job experience to see how people actually act in a pot-limit poker game. Furthermore, a certain action may mean something different, depending on who does it. Perhaps Johnny Jones bets with a slight flourish when he's bluffing, but Suzy Smith has a rockcrusher when she uses that type of betting motion. Even so, we think you can improve your skills in reading people to some degree by listening to the right type of advice.

Big-bet poker differs from most limit poker games in that the amount a player may bet is flexible rather than fixed. The size of the bet conveys information about the bettor's hand. Interpreting this information is not easy, because there is no simple formula that applies to all people, situations, or types of poker. A big bet may mean a big hand. It can also be an indication of fear. Perhaps the bettor is bluffing. But more often, he simply has a hand that he thinks is good, yet is easily catchable. He wants you to fold. A couple of examples are a pair of jacks at hold'em before the flop, or a pat 8-7-6-5-4 at Ace-to-Five lowball draw.

An unusually small bet can be a light probe by a weak hand. It could also mean a big hand looking for action. For example, suppose a lowball draw player opens in early position for the absolute minimum, then stands pat. Watch out! Most pat hand holders open with a fairly large bet, because they don't want you to draw against them cheaply. So beware of Greeks bearing gifts. Getting a great price for your one-card draw may mean you are drawing dead or close to it, up against a pat six or wheel.

I remember a pot-limit Omaha hand where a former World Champion put in a big reraise before the flop, which looked a lot like two double-suited aces. His inexperienced opponent called heads-up out of position. There was about fifteen hundred dollars in the pot preflop. Both players still had plenty of money in front of them. The flop came A♣-9♠-4♠. The weak player checked and the W.C. bet a small bet in relation to the pot size, and also quite out of character for the bettor, who usually bet the full size of the pot. All of us experienced players knew exactly what had happened. The W.C. had flopped a huge hand; top set and the nut flush-draw. The cheap bet was a Greek gift. His opponent did not understand the situation. The unfortunate fellow called the bet, drew at the flush, and made the mistake of hitting it on fourth street. When the smoke cleared, he had lost his entire stack of six thousand dollars. A small bet at a big pot could be a weak probe, but when a habitually heavy gunner does it, there might be big trouble lurking for the would-be caller.

How do you detect a bluff after all the cards are out? One important principle is a player who has a little something to show down seldom resorts to a bluff. He simply checks and sees if his hand is good. Bluffing is an act of the desperate. Someone who has absolutely nothing is much more likely to bluff than a player who has some kind of hand. A hold'em player drawing at a jack-high straight and missing is far more likely to bluff than a player holding A-K who was trying to make a pair and missed. A lowball draw player who took one card is more likely to bluff if he busted out by pairing a six than by catching a queen or king.

I have seen players get check-raised on the end and call, hoping to catch a bluff. While a bluff here is not impossible, it is certainly improbable. If an opponent had nothing and wanted to run a bluff, he is much more likely to lead into you instead of check-raising. How could he be sure you would bet?

Mannerisms that give away the strength of your hand are called "tells." Poker literature discusses many of these tells, always with the same principle in mind. Players try to fool you. If they are strong they act weak, and vice-versa. My experience is this shows up most often in a player's betting tempo. A fast bet may be a bluff, whereas a slow, hesitating bet may be a powerhouse. However, there are quite a few exceptions to this. So it pays to watch people and see what their normal betting tempo is, and what it means if they are abnormally fast or slow.

This tendency for poker players to act the opposite of what they really feel is reflected in how they play a big hand. Quite a few players habitually slowplay their big hands. Try to identify players with this penchant, and take advantage of this knowledge.

Here are a few mannerisms and what they usually mean:

(1) Shaking hands come more often from the excitement of holding a good hand than the nervousness of a bluff.

(2) A player who reaches for his money as you are about to bet would prefer that you checked. He may still call, but is unlikely to have a big hand.

(3) Beware of "speech bets." A player who bets with his mouth yapping may well be chirping because of the excitement of holding a good hand.

(4) A player who checks out-of-turn when the flop came down may be excited because he just hit a whopper.

(5) A player who looks at his money and then checks was thinking about betting.

(6) I find that a player who acts a little disgusted when he checks on the end, if it is not a total act, will still remain with a good enough hand to call if you bet. For example, a hold'em hand for this action might be top pair with the nut flush-draw. He is disappointed that he missed the flush, but he still has a pair of aces.

We have only scratched the surface of the subject of reading the opponent. To develop your skill in this department, be observant of your opponents. Pay particular attention to how much they like to bet in certain situations and the tempo used for the bet. Each player has his own "signature," although this will vary with whether he is in front or stuck for that session. If you notice an unusual mannerism, do not automatically assign it the meaning it had when someone else did it. We all have individual idiosyncrasies, and you must learn what it means when that particular player acts in such a manner.

We'll close this chapter with a couple of warnings. First, a loose gambling player will have times when he is simply not in the mood to play fast, so don't automatically pay him off. Second, when you're stuck, don't rely so heavily on some mannerism that you start finding flimsy excuses to make bad calls.

ADDENDUM BY STEWART

The real reason this chapter has to be limited in scope, despite the fact that there is little of more importance than going to the library in big-bet poker, is that it can't be taught. It is mostly experience and "feel." This cannot be explained.

I once had a hand against a certain fellow at seven stud; I bet and he raised all-in. This could only be justified if he held one specific card in his hand. I called "knowing" he didn't have it. The look on his face when he hit this precise card was almost worth the fact I lost the pot.

Jackie once went all in against me at seven-card stud with an open pair of 8s. So dead were his cards that I knew he couldn't be full. After much thought, I called with aces with one card to come. "Full house," he said. "No, you haven't," was my response. He had two pair and I improved to out-draw him.

Tony is a good player. The flop was Q-7-4 at Omaha. I held kings. The hand was checked on the flop with Tony last to speak. Now there came an 8. Everybody checked to Tony. He bet and I raised with just that pair. "Call," he said. Last card led to a board of Q 7 4 8 4. I checked and Tony checked, saying he had a straight. "No, you don't," was my riposte. He looked at his hand and conceded I was right. Unfortunately, he had a 4 in his hand and thus won. He is still annoyed I knew better than him what he held.

Please feel free to explain these things to me. I suppose, in the last example, I felt Tony wouldn't check in last position with four to an up-and-down nut straight. Yet, these are three examples in 25 years play where I knew **better** than my opponent what they had in the hole. Even so, I am regarded as one of the most rational players.

IRRATIONAL PLAY

Sometimes a play is made which doesn't make sense. This has little effect at limit poker as it can be ignored, but in big-bet poker the reverberations can be substantial.

As an example, recently in limit seven card stud I had (Q♥ 2♥) 8♥ K♥. I was high and checked to two other players. The first player bet and both the other player and I called. On fifth street (Q♥ 2♥) 8♥ K♥ 6♣ and I was still high. Now I bet. Both players called. Card six I again bet and received two calls. On the river, I made the flush, bet out and received two calls. They stared blankly at my hand when revealed, until I put them out of their misery and told them the 6♣ was totally irrelevant.

Of course, it looked as if that six had helped me. If I hit an 8 or 6 on sixth street, there would have been a very fair chance I would win the pot there and then. In addition, a heart on sixth street is less likely to put on the frighteners.

At pot-limit my opponent was high with an open pair in seven stud. He bet, and I with a flush raised. He called and then came out, perfectly obviously, betting blind on the river. What was I to make of this? Anyway, I called and won. Some months later I tried the same trick when I had a full house. My opponent passed. Of course, he probably didn't notice my bizarre play.

In Omaha there are several people in the pot and the flop shows A-10-7. Everybody checks. Now fourth street up pops a 2 and a player decides to bet early in hand. How could the deuce be relevant? The answer, of course, is that it almost certainly isn't; the previous three cards were the important ones.

Generally you should treat irrational plays as acts containing no inherent information. After all, your opponent may be drunk or stoned!

MULTIWAY POTS

Hands in which there are more than two participants can provide splendid opportunities for a good read.

At sixth street in seven-card stud a player has bet with (? ?) A 4 9 A. You called with two pair and a third party did likewise with (? ?) K 9 7 J. On the river, the first player goes all-in. It is inconceivable that the other opponent has less than kings up. A pass is required. Occasionally, it is possible to call with just two pair in the belief the aces are bluffing. I have even managed this myself at limit poker. With your call you are actually bluffing the third player in the hand. His kings up must pass and you can scoop in a substantial pot with a ridiculous holding. This smacks of black magic and is likely to put that third player on tilt.

Again it is seven stud. You hold (Q 9) Q 8 2 4 with all your cards splattered liberally around the table. Your sole opponent is a strong player. You bet and he raises. A call is in order and a call at the river if he bets. If both queens have fallen, so much the better. You can call blind. He is probably on a steal.

Once again, it is seven stud. You hold (A♣ 7♣) 9♣ 4♣. The pot is checked to you, and all the nines and fours have passed. You bet and are raised. Raise again. He is trying to push you over with a dead hand.

At London lowball, the high card has acted and three players each with a 2 call. You hold (A 2) 3 and raise the pot. The next player with a 6 calls. All the others pass. Card 4 (A 2) 3 6 and your strong opponent (? ?) 6 A now comes out betting the pot. He is reading you for a 6 in the hole. Now raise the maximum. You will never have such an advantageous situation. Now, if he is reading in comfort and leisure, he should be able to work out you have the case 2. This pot actually occurred, and my much-respected opponent called holding (8 4) 6 A. It was virtually all-in. He reckoned 2-1 for his money was a fair shot. In fact, against this holding, he is in dire straits. At least, he waited a card before the total plunge. Had I hit the case 2, then he can pass no matter how large the pot and small the bet.

Players often overlook the fact that they are at the same library as their opponents. What is clear to them may be equally transparent to the opposition. Do please be a literate player.

11-THE ART OF BLUFFING
by Bob Ciaffone

Bluffing is a tool of great importance to big-bet poker players. Being able to bet the size of the pot means a lot of bets go uncalled. Good judgment about whether to run a bluff will result in winning plenty of money. What are some indications that a successful bluff can be launched?

This sounds trite, but it is important to realize that the purpose of a bluff is to win the pot. Some players think the main purpose of bluffing is to set up situations to make money by getting your good hands paid off. Bluffs will have the fringe benefit of helping you make money on strong hands, but this should be treated only as a byproduct of bluffing. Players who are too conscious of the advertising value of a bluff tend to overwork this play. Launch a bluff when you think it will be successful, and let the advertising take care of itself.

The less often you bluff, the more successful your bluffs will be. Opponents do watch how you play, and a tight image means fewer calls. It is up to each player to find the amount of bluffing that works best for his style of play. This desirable bluffing ratio will vary from session to session. If you're holding good hands and winning a lot of pots by uncalled bets, the opponents may well think you are running bluffs. Be careful about bluffing when your exceptionally good cards already make it look like you're trying to run over the game. And for heaven's sake, don't show those hands unless forced to by a call.

Some people are harder to bluff than others. Weak players tend to call more. A player having a losing session is more apt to talk himself into a call than a winner would be. People who are wealthy tend to put money into the pot more often than average people. Particularly prone to calling are players who have a lot of cash, such as bookmakers, bar owners, and drug dealers. It pays to think about who you are bluffing.

Sometimes the cards you hold indicate that a bluff will have a better than usual chance of success. Here are a few examples:

(1) At Omaha, there are three of a suit on board creating a possible flush, and you hold the lone ace of that suit.

(2) At hold'em, the board is K-9-8-6-3, and you hold pocket sevens, the key card needed for the straight.

(3) At lowball draw, you pick up 3-3-3-2-2, five low cards that others will need.

(4) At seven-card stud, you have a deuce showing, and an ace and king of that suit in the hole. A player in late position with an ace showing raises your forced lowcard bet.

Position plays an important role in bluffing strategy. If the other players all check to you, sometimes it pays to take them at their word. After all, the odds favor them being weak, rather than slipping a good hand to you. Poker hands good enough to be planning a check-raise are not that easy to come by.

Big-bet poker differs greatly from limit poker in the frequency with which players initially check, and then call or raise when someone in late position bets. Big-bet players back in much less often. In a no-limit hold'em or pot-limit Omaha game you should be picking up threeway pots with a bet at least half the time when the opponents check. And if you check in first position and the field checks behind you, think about picking up the pot with a bet on the next round if the new boardcard looks innocuous. You must not let money sit in the pot to rot.

A bluff that represents a specific holding has a better chance of success than money that simply says, "I like my hand." When that third card to a flush hits on the board at hold'em, a bet says, "I have a flush." You don't figure to get called unless the opponent has a flush himself, or can hit either a bigger flush or a full house on the next card. At Omaha, if the board pairs, a player who is drawing to a straight or flush will lose interest in the pot. This is a good time to make a small bet and find out what you're up against.

An important principle in bluffing is that a relatively small amount of money threatens the opponent with a large loss if you have the hand you are representing. If you bet a thousand dollars all-in, this does not apply nearly as much pressure as when there is still several thousand dollars left that the opponent may need to put into the pot to see the hand through. This is one reason why top big-bet players prefer to buy in for a goodly sum of money.

When you bluff, let the bet itself do the work of scaring your opponent out of the pot. Do not try to bet in a confident manner. Do not say anything. Do not try to stare down the opposition. These extra flourishes are liable to produce the opposite result to the one you desire. If you have chosen the right opponent and situation for a bluff, he is quite likely to fold. Don't give him an excuse to make a long call.

Don't be afraid to bluff when you first take up big-bet poker. Experiment a little bit to see what you can get away with. At any form of poker, you should not be playing a lot of starting hands. This will give you the image of a tight player. This image will give your bluffs a good chance of success, so make it work for you.

12-BEATING THE BULLY
by Bob Ciaffone and Stewart Reuben

PART 1—BY BOB

Many a poker game has a player in it who constantly puts pressure on the other players by betting and raising. At limit he can be combated by simply waiting for a good hand and then picking him off. At big-bet poker, if you wait too long, you may be backed into your shell for the whole game. On the other hand, if you find yourself in many big pots with inadequate values, you can be taken to the cleaners.

Here are some ways of dealing with the threat of the bully:

(1) Avoid short-handed play. Bulldozing tactics are more effective with few players at the table. The bully will be in his element in a five-handed game; at nine-handed he will not be nearly as big a problem.

(2) Play fewer starting hands. Because the bully is playing everything under the sun, it is tempting to follow suit. A better way of thinking is, "The pot is quite likely to be raised, so I need a better hand to enter into the action."

(3) Don't let the bully run you into the nuts. Remember, to win the pot, you must beat everybody in play, not just him. Often it is better to call his bet rather than raise, holding a decent but not exceptional hand, if there are players behind you yet to act, or even who have already checked.

Where to sit with such a player in the game is a matter of debate. My view is the worst is to the bully's immediate left. You have position on him and can put a great deal of pressure on the other players with a double raise, but you'll get run into good hands held by other players too much. There are several different kinds of bully. One who automatically bets every time you check is a person you are less in need of having position on. I don't mind being to the right of such a player. I prefer to be sitting across from one who shows you a lot of moves (if I must play in his game). This gives me a view of how the pot is going to develop, and I will have position on the bully about half the time. There are some poker writers who disagree with this, but for how many decades have they been playing pot-limit Omaha with O'Neil Longson or no-limit hold'em with the late Bill Smith?

(4) Don't pull the trigger too soon when you are lucky enough to snag a big hand against the bully. Check and call may well be superior to check-and-raise in many situations. It is necessary to run the risk of being outdrawn in order to teach the bully that "check" is not synonymous with "I'm weak."

(5) Normally, you should wait for a hand with nut outs before putting a play on somebody. Three may be adequate. This gives you the chance of winning the pot there-and-then or making your hand. But against the bully you may wish to run a cold bluff, because your chance of catching him completely out-of-line are pretty good. You've got to fight fire with fire. Basically, you cannot let a bully continually push you into the corner. You've got to take a stand. Give him a dose of his own medicine once in a while. He's not likely to be holding a hand that can take the heat.

PART 2—BY STEWART

Bob asked me to add my views on this topic, but hyper-aggressive opponents picking on me is not a problem I have to face very often; more the other way around. Perhaps that is why he suggested it; to make me a poacher turned gamekeeper.

An opponent who just bets with any old hand in a ring game isn't too hard to beat. Just wait until you have a good hand and pounce. Others in the game will do the same, so that each pot becomes head-up between the bully and one other player. He may devastate you—in fact this is a certainty sometimes—but you should just grit your teeth, smile and plod on. All aggressive players, however wild and unsound, are dangerous. Give me the soft, weak player any day.

If you are up against a strong, very aggressive player, things aren't so easy. Sometimes you should bet into him or raise him on a bluff. You are trying to take the steal-play away from him. It can be good to appear defensive. Then, when you take action on your moderate hands, you are more likely to get a great deal of respect, and people will pass. Great hands don't fly in every hour, so don't worry excessively about failing to get the money in early when you have a bone-cruncher.

When up against somebody you fear, don't be afraid of acknowledging this to yourself. Maintaining the correct psychological stance is an immensely important facet of good poker play. It will be best to steer clear of this opponent and tackle pots with the live ones. There is something to be said for sitting to the immediate left of the tiger and passing when he takes action. When in a pot with him, don't try to be fancy. Just play the odds and raise the maximum when you are winning but are frightened of an out-draw. This fear isn't due to the fact that he may win the pot, but because you may have to face a big bet and there is no way of knowing whether he is bluffing. If you always pass, what a joy for the bully. If you always call, he'll notice. I was playing in a pot and my bluff was called. A player who had just lost an even bigger pot to me turned to his girlfriend and whispered, "You see, it's impossible to tell what he's got." Of course, that's why I never bluffed him. He always called because he could see other occasions where I was at it.

Alec Polski adopted the simple system against me of always checking his strong hands to me. Then, when I bet assuming he was weak, he raised. When I cottoned on to this, I stopped betting with junk and drawing hands. Now I was sometimes getting a free card. Varying your play is essential in poker. Sometimes I would check my powerhouse straight back to him. Then the peculiar situation would arise that conflagration took place much later in the pot than you would have expected.

In America particularly, some players seek to intimidate you physically, verbally or with money. It is no bad thing to appear to lie down under this. Eventually they will find out their mistake— too late. Mike Caro's "Book of Tells" constantly reiterates the fact that strong means weak and a weak representation means strong. Unfortunately, now so many people are clued up on this, it isn't such a giveaway. A significant minority of players not only want to win your money, but also to crush your ego. Thus they tell you they are strong, bet strong, and by golly, are strong. Then, when you call, they crow with delight, "Told you so."

Seven stud presents excellent bullying prospects in pot-limit. If your opponents' boards look weak and they have shown weakness, it is perfectly possible to bet them out irrespective of your own holding. It is good to set the scene early in the hand. Thus I am happy to make a small bet on fourth street with (6 6) 4 Q in a multihanded action pot. Few will raise me with weakish hands because they are frightened of generating a huge pot. I can switch off on fifth street if necessary, or try to powerhouse my way through, frequently successfully.

Effectively my small wager is increasing the size of the game. Only relatively sophisticated players seem to understand my action results in a bigger game without the need to pay increased table money or play with a bigger ante. I am first building the pot and **then** building my hand. As the pot continues, the size of the pot is tremendously increased. I try to think only in terms of percentage of the pot; others think of the actual sum at risk. Thus they become nervous and more prone to error.

I remember one player in pot-limit Omaha who used to delight in making a small wager after the flop with weak hands. It became my habit to sit to his immediate left. Then, after his bet came an instant raise from me, unless I had a strong hand. One day, disaster struck. A third party called. The original bettor passed and the pot was checked out. As those were the rules, I had to show my miserable holding. He visibly started, and that was the end of that. He was much too strong to fail to pick up on what I had been doing.

Clearly the bully problem is exacerbated in games such as draw or hold'em where you have less data to go on. Eventually you must make a stand against the bully, you cannot simply let him run all over you. But presumably you are playing in a ring game and have other matters on your mind than this particular confrontation. Thus I cannot agree with Doyle Brunson, who writes in the excellent book "Power-play" that he will choose to fight back with virtually any hand. He may as well raise blind. Surely you can choose a battlefield more to your taste than that?

Both Bob and I have expressed considerable concern about our position at the table relative to other players. Frankly, these days my main concern is to avoid the smokers. {Ditto!-Bob} Financial considerations are purely secondary. Since the first edition of our book was printed, smoking has mercifully been banned from California cardrooms. I live in the hope that smoking will be prohibited in most Vegas casinos within a few years. {Another ditto!}

13-NO-LIMIT PLAY
by Bob Ciaffone

No-limit poker means just what it says; you can bet all your chips at once, if you fancy. Of course, in both pot-limit and no-limit, you may only bet what you have on the table (the Table Stakes rule).

No-limit poker has certain advantages over pot-limit. The most important one is no bookkeeping is necessary. You don't have to keep track of the pot size, and police the game so the pot is not overbet. Some players prefer no-limit because they feel there is a better chance of getting the opponent's entire stack of chips. There is also a certain macho element, as if no-limit were the ultimate test of courage.

There are some drawbacks to no-limit play. In the early going, overbetting the pot tends to kill the action instead of promoting it. When there is $50 in the pot and someone lets fly with a $200 bet, this usually ends matters. If it doesn't, a $1,000 reraise figures to get the job done.

In poker, there is greater opportunity for skill in reading the opponent if we can observe him over several betting rounds. Top players prefer a pot that builds in increments instead of one big explosion. Then you have more information in reaching a decision.

There are major differences between the forms of poker in their suitability for no-limit betting. For example, lowball draw seems to lend itself quite well to no-limit. There are only two betting rounds, and it is most unlikely someone will have the nuts (a wheel) before the draw.

Omaha is a good example of a game that is better played at pot-limit betting. There are four betting rounds, and as soon as the flop is spread, someone can have the (temporary) nuts. A player with that holding has a tendency to want to overbet the pot by a ton, enough to shut out the opposition. The intricate play as a pot grows with each betting round will be gone. When big-bet style Omaha was first introduced to Las Vegas in 1983, it was played at no-limit betting. Within a week, the better players preferred to switch to pot-limit betting. Ever since, the game has been pot-limit Omaha.

Hold'em is a poker form that often uses either pot-limit or no-limit betting. It is a lot harder to get the nuts at hold'em than Omaha, so that objection to no-limit is much reduced. The biggest objection to no-limit play for cash games (as opposed to tournaments) is the extra intimidation of weaker players, who don't like to have their entire stack of chips put at risk very often. We need to keep weaker players in our game.

Every pot-limit player ought to learn no-limit play. First, it is an easy step. (Going from limit to pot-limit is much more difficult.) Second, the premier event at many poker tournaments is no-limit hold'em. And, of course, the World Championship is contested at that style of play.

There are several major differences between no-limit play and pot-limit play. First, it is common for the pot to be overbet when it is small. Second, position play is somewhat different. Third, it is important to know when to overbet the pot, whether you are drawing or have a made hand. Let's discuss these points a bit.

Every no-limit game has its own tempo. But most games tend to have players lean on the antes a lot by overbetting the pot. For example, at lowball draw with a $25 ante and one $50 blind, a seven-handed game will initially have $225 in the pot. The average opening bet will usually be about $300. In a $5-$10-$25 blind no-limit hold'em game, a player opening with a raise will often make the wager $150 or $200, and sometimes more. This contrasts with the maximum figure of $100 that would be allowable at pot-limit hold'em (after rounding off the pot size).

Obviously, if the pot odds are less favorable at no-limit than pot-limit, your standards for initial involvement have to be a little higher. So in raised pots, you need quite a good hand to play.

Since raising by overbetting the pot-size is more likely to win it right away, there is more bluffing at no-limit. Whether you yourself should do more bluffing initially depends on your style of play. But every no-limit player has to learn when to play back at a muscle-the-antes player. You need to reraise on occasion without having the values, to keep certain people from running over you.

For example, at no-limit hold'em you get a hand actually worth a reraise before the flop only a few times a session. If most pots are getting bombarded, you need to do something about it. Waiting for a big pair to play back may lead to hours of frustration. So you need to put a play on those bombardiers once in a while.

At hold'em, the ante-stealer can stand to get called before the flop by your light but hopeful hand. He likely will bet the flop, and it's about 2-to-1 you won't have a pair (unless you started with one). So the way to take the wind out of his sails is to reraise on those hands you were thinking about calling. Fight fire with fire.

Position play at no-limit is a little different than pot-limit. The more betting rounds there are, the more important position becomes. You would rather have position on someone for each betting round, not just one or two. When out of position with a through ticket you want to get all-in as fast as possible. Having position on someone who is all-in will be absolutely worthless. When you are allowed to overbet the pot and scoot your whole stack, people will get all-in at earlier stages of the play than they would at pot-limit, so good position is not quite as valuable. (Position at no-limit is still far more important than at limit poker.)

At pot-limit, having a drawing hand up front is very bad. The thing you want to avoid is getting a quarter or half of your money in out-of-position against an opponent who strongly suspects you are drawing. Your adversary is likely to get away from his hand if you hit and move in, and will set you all-in if you miss and check. It would be better if you had the option of moving all-in yourself before there was (for example) only one card to come. At no-limit you have that option, and should use it when holding a big draw out-of-position—and sometimes in position. So you can play potential drawing cards in no-limit more often than in pot-limit, but don't overdo it. Only use this as a way to vary your play, not as a steady diet.

Knowing when to overbet the pot and move all-in is very important at no-limit. The big draw out-of-position is one common situation. Another is with a good made hand if you fear "losing your market." For example, suppose in a no-limit hold'em game you flop a set of trips against an early raiser who usually has his values.

The flop comes 10♣-9♣-3♠, and he bets into your three nines. This is a good spot to overbet the pot and move in. He likely has an overpair. The next card may well make a possible straight or flush, and cause him to have some doubts about the strength of his hand. Now is the time to put the question to him. Those drawing cards on the board may well cause him to misread the situation and call.

What if your opponent has three tens? In that case, you are almost surely going to lose all your money. But you can't play no-limit poker by waiting for the nuts with no cards to come before committing your whole stack. As long as you are still in the game, those chips are in front of you to use for betting or raising. If you are viewing them as money to buy something other than a pot, it is time to cash out.

Finally, it is important at no-limit in certain other situations to overbet the pot and move all-in on an opponent who is drawing, when you have a made hand. This can be done, of course, when a mere pot-size bet would be giving an opponent an attractive price, but an overbet changes the odds enough to compel a fold. It is certainly not automatic to make a huge bet any time you are pretty sure he is drawing. There are times when you would prefer to leave him in the pot paying a price to continue. For example, it is possible a number of his "outs" could get him to lose a bundle because they actually make you a better hand.

Overbetting the pot and moving all-in against a draw has its reward even if the opponent can call. A drawing hand with money left to bet has betting leverage, which increases the opponent's equity in the pot beyond the straight-forward odds of completing the draw. This is called his "implied odds." We seldom can be certain whether the opponent has what he is representing. Sometimes we err and pay him off, and other times we err by folding when he has bluffed. When the draw is all-in, you do not need to play guessing games with him. For a detailed discussion of this situation—which is also relevant to pot-limit play—see the chapter "Important Pot-limit Concepts," which follows our London Lowball chapter.

At pot-limit we find that a big bet does not always show a big hand. The extra money wagered over an average-size bet may be added out of fear. The bettor may be trying to shut you out or rob you. This applies even more to no-limit, which has an even stronger intimidation factor. You have got to know your situations, and especially your players.

There is a lot to no-limit play, far more than can be covered in a single chapter. However, the concepts we are teaching you about pot-limit can in nearly all cases be applied to no-limit. Since you are already investing time and money to learn pot-limit play, we recommend you take that little extra step and learn no-limit as well. It's worth your while.

14-ALL IN COUPS
by Stewart Reuben

Where there are more than two people in the pot, as soon as one is all-in, this leads to a sidepot in which the all-in player has no interest. If the tapped player is first to speak in a stud game, the betting in England then proceeds to the next-best hand showing. In America it proceeds clockwise from the all-in player. The English system is better poker.

Only when a player is going all-in is he allowed to under-raise in a multihanded pot. This under-raise cannot be used to make a further raise. Thus Player A bets $100, Player B calls, Player C raises $20 all-in. Now neither A nor B can reraise. D can do whatever he wants. I believe it is unethical to use a player's small all-in bet to take further action in a given round. The pot is $100. Player A checks, Player B checks, C now goes all-in for $20. Player A calls and now B raises. It isn't against the rules but that don't make it right. A good rule might be that a player's all-in bet cannot be used to take action if that bet is less than 50% of the minimum buy-in. {Note from Bob; most American cardrooms use the rule that a wager must be at least the size of the minimum bring-in to reopen the betting to a player who has already acted.}

Gruesome things can happen if you are not careful, due to the artificial nature of a situation where a player has no money left. Seven-card stud. Ken (? ? ?) 7 9 4 2. Alf (? ? ?) Q 6 8 2. John, all-in (? ? ?) A J 6 J. Adam (J 7 ?) 10 Q A 8. The pot was $1000. Adam knew he had bought the straight; there was no sidepot and he bet $500. Ken and Alf each gave it a long think and each passed reluctantly. Adam triumphantly showed his "straight," but it turned to ashes. To his dismay, he had bought another 7, not a 9. He couldn't beat the open jacks, which was all John held. Now all hell broke loose. Ken claimed he had been pushed out with trip nines, and Alf claimed to have held trip eights. Of course John had to win the pot, as neither Ken nor Alf had any cards at all. Alf should have tried to hold onto his hand until the others had shown down. Even if there had been a side pot of just $50, Adam's bet would have been legal—albeit a bit mischievous—to deprive players of their chance to win the whole for such scant reward.

I was reproached about my actions in the following London lowball hand. The pot size was $10K. I had (A 2) 3 7 10 J. Ed (? ?) 2 9 Q 5. Gerry (? ?) A 8 8 K. Ed had only $500 left. I bet $10K, Ed called and Gerry passed. Ed's 9 low stood up. Now Gerry complained bitterly I had pushed him out of the pot when losing to Ed. This doesn't stand up. Had I checked, Ed bet his $500, Gerry called, and then I raised, that would indeed be unethical. But Ed could have paired up. It is unlikely he has an 8 in the hole, four to a 9-8 being such a poor hand. Thus he has two of A 3 4 5 6 7 in the hole. His latest upcard pairing a 5 in the hole can be expected 32% of the time. Also I didn't want to let Gerry into the pot on sixth street, only for me to improve to an 8 low and find he has made a better one. If he has four to a good low, let him call; my 10 made is a winning proposition for the sidepot.

In an Omaha coup I had J-10-9-6 double-suited. We were threehanded and there had been a blind bet and a raise before the flop, which came K-Q-5. The pot was $4000 and I went all-in for this sum. The original raiser, Donnacha O'Dea, dwelt and passed his aces. The other player called all-in for $200 and won the pot with a pair of kings, as the last two cards didn't improve me. Donnacha is one of the very best and most ethical players, but he still hasn't forgiven me for bluffing him out, allowing a virtually all-in player to win. But my action gave me 11 outs in two cards to win the pot, about a 46% chance, for only $200. Had I checked, the aces might have set me in, and obviously I am less than even money. Had he checked and then I checked on fourth street, he would probably have bet. Then my excellent odds would have been in tatters. A check would only have gained if we both check on the flop, an ace comes on fourth street, I check, and he goes all-in without improving on the river. Omaha is a peculiar game in that it is commonplace to have a drawing hand close to 50% or even higher. No, my play stands up to the closest scrutiny.

15-USING THE MATERIAL
by Stewart and Bob

In this section of our book we discuss the specific forms of poker. Covered are hold'em, Omaha, seven-card stud, lowball draw, London lowball, and high-low split eight-or-better. Some of these games are usually played pot-limit, and others no-limit. The main adjustments the pot-limit player must make in no-limit play is knowing when to overbet the pot size, and recognizing when he is being charged too much money to stay in the pot. However, the principles of play are similar, so for games like hold'em and lowball that are played with either betting structure, we compress both betting structures into the same chapter.

As you read, pay close attention to the pot size and amount of money in front of the players whenever a decision is made. The right play on a big-bet poker hand heavily depends on these factors.

We strongly urge you to read about all the poker forms, including the ones you have no interest in playing, to get the maximum out of the book. It is likely that some valuable ideas will be discussed in one poker form that can be applied to another. Also, by seeing a concept applied to several different games, you can better understand and remember it.

Be sure to read the chapter called "Important Pot-limit Concepts." We have elected to place it directly following the London Lowball chapter because the ideas are presented in a London Lowball setting, and directly related to some scenarios portrayed in that chapter.

Each major chapter is followed by a quiz on the presented material. The score for each answer is given in brackets. You may not be interested in all games, but we recommend you look at each question. The point considered may be relevant to more than one game. Add up your score in each section; the total assesses your ability to play theoretically in each game. Anytime you make a choice which is awarded a negative score, you have really made a ghastly play. We feel quizzes are a useful tool for measuring your progress and deciding whether you are "combat ready."

16-POT-LIMIT & NO-LIMIT HOLD'EM
"How Deep The Money Is Determines Your Play"

by Bob Ciaffone

Pot-limit and no-limit and hold'em are so closely related—both are what we call "big-bet poker"—that the strategies we talk about in this chapter apply to both forms unless specifically stated otherwise. The only difference in rules between the two betting structures is no-limit allows you to overbet the pot size.

No-limit hold'em has been called by two-time World Champion Doyle Brunson "The Cadillac of poker games." The grand finale event at most poker tournaments is played at this demanding game. It calls for aggressiveness, patience, and skill at reading the opponent. The same can be said for pot-limit hold'em.

Most people are familiar with limit hold'em. Let's compare limit poker with big-bet poker and see how it affects our starting hands. At limit play, turning a super-class hand like a set will win you an extra couple of bets. At big-bet the upside is far greater. You can double through the opponent, winning a pot from two to twelve times the size of an average pot, perhaps even greater. Hands that can win a big pot are worth more.

A pair of aces are a fine hand at any form of hold 'em, but they are even nicer at big-bet. However, it must be emphasized that their most important function is to get all-in before the flop against K-K, Q-Q, A-K, and any other hand that an opponent may play strongly at this point. Since it is easier to get all-in at no-limit than pot-limit, aces are at their best in a no-limit structure. After the flop, unimproved aces seem to bust the holder as often as the enemy, so there you should tread carefully with only one pair.

Actually, any pair is more valuable at big-bet poker than at limit play, because a concealed set is the classic hand for doubling up. Of course, you need to start with a pair to make a concealed set. Once you flop a set, it is a very hard hand to turn loose. Even though set over set is rare, it is so expensive to be on the lower end that small pairs are a double-edged proposition. I recommend playing deuces through fives only in late position and unraised pots.

The nut flush is a fine hand for the purpose of getting doubled up. There is something about a flush that makes the cards stick to your hand, and many a player has lost his stack by getting married to a non-nut flush. Therefore, a suited ace is a better hand at big-bet poker than limit play. Even so, it still usually needs an accompanying big card to participate in a raised pot.

Keep in mind that although hands like 7-7 or a suited ace are worth more at big-bet poker, the entry price to a raised pot is many times greater than at limit play. Since these hands need improvement to contend after the flop, and you are an underdog to help, avoid being overcharged to see the flop. We discuss this later.

If pairs and suited aces are worth more at no-limit, something has got to be worth less. That something is big unsuited cards. Hands with an offsuit A-K, A-Q, and K-Q are used at limit play for making top pair with a good kicker. That hand is okay at big-bet poker for winning a small pot—or losing a big one. Since getting doubled up is what we aim for, these hands are dangerous. Don't back top pair with all your money unless forced to by a very high ante structure.

Another place big-bet differs from limit is the importance of position. At limit play, good position lets you trap someone for an extra bet or steal a small pot. At big-bet, good position lets you trap someone for his whole stack or steal a large pot. Position is a far more important factor when the money is deep in relation to the blinds and ante structure. For example, suppose each player has a grand in chips. Position assumes more importance with blinds of $5-$5-$10 than blinds of $50-$50-$100. The former situation lets you use a positional advantage on each betting round, instead of simply deciding whether to go all-in before the flop.

When people talk about "position," they usually are referring to the privilege of acting later or last on a betting round; in other words, being on or near the button. There is another form of position that has great importance at big-bet hold'em. That is having good position in relation to the raiser.

At hold'em, a raising-quality hand is often good enough to bet the flop without improving. Here hold'em differs markedly from Omaha. Even if the hand is not actually that strong, the raiser often bets the flop anyway, judging by the preflop betting action that the opposition may be weak. If an ace or king comes, the raiser bets to portray A-K (which he may well have). If the board comes with small, unrelated cards, he bets to portray an overpair (which he also may well have). At any rate, the preflop aggressor normally will bet after the flop well over half the time. You, the caller, want to have the best possible position to take advantage of this.

It is obvious that in multihanded pots you want the raiser betting through the field of players into you. Therefore, the best placement is to be on the button (or have last action) when someone has raised under the gun or in the blind position. This is obvious. What may not be so obvious is that if is someone raises in late position or on the button and others call, you want to be on the raiser's right. This way, if everyone checks to him, his bet will put the others in the middle, and you will have the commanding position. If the others check the flop and you decide to bet a marginal hand or a bluff, there is the additional leverage against the raiser of the other players who checked, and the raiser will seldom get involved without solid values.

Note that if you are on the button and the raiser is on your immediate right, your position is actually shaky. If the raiser bets the flop, the bet puts you in the middle. If someone has checked a strong hand expecting the raiser to bet, they bag you as well. Sometimes the raiser checks the flop, but this is not as helpful with the raiser on your right, as anybody could have checked a bushwhacker expecting the raiser to bet. Note the huge difference from when the raiser has early position and is first to act and checks, and the others also check. In a threeway or fourway pot, this situation is so favorable for a steal it is tempting to fire with any holding. The raiser nearly always has missed the flop and decided not to bluff. The others, knowing this, still do not care to bet, so they are unlikely to have even a modest hand. You will only get called or raised if someone is slowplaying a monster, or there is a "policeman" or "calling station" in the game.

This is a good time to discuss how to play against a habitual caller. They come in two basic types. The first type is liable to call off his entire stack when you continue firing at him. The way to play against him is simply to wait for a good hand and milk him. The second type is the guy who assumes you are weak unless you fire a second barrel at him. He will call you on the flop (or on fourth street if the flop was checked and you now bet) just to see if you have anything, or to hit some longshot draw. It is important to fire that second barrel to brush this sort of sand flea off you.

Back when I lived in Dallas and no-limit hold' em was my bread and butter, a poker-playing friend asked me what I thought was the strongest part of my game. My reply was, "Knowing when to fire that second barrel." The best advice I can give an aspiring big-bet hold'em player is to get to know his opponent's betting habits, and how they like to handle the many different situations where someone bets into them, they call, and the opponent bets again. The winner must be able to distinguish between a perpetual caller and a look-up artist. Brush off those sand fleas!

There is a situation where I am reluctant to fire a second barrel. If I raise the pot, an ace (or king) comes, and I bet, this "announces" A-K. When someone calls me, assuming there is no flush-draw on board, either he does not believe I have A-K, or he can beat it. Either way, another bet by me is a huge favorite to get called. I feel a player foolish enough to call a preflop raise with a weak-kicker ace and then call again when the raiser bets the flop is likely to continue calling. So once you diagram A-K by raising preflop and betting the flop, it is better to cut your losses and abandon ship if you are bluffing and someone is still fighting.

When there is a flush-draw on the board, and you bet on the flop and get called, you have (against most players) undertaken a commitment. If the flush is not completed on fourth street, it is necessary to fire again. If you are bluffing, follow through; if you have a marginal hand, fire and hope for the best; if you have a good hand, by all means protect it. The only things that would stop me from betting would be: (1) I have been called by a perpetual caller (2) I want to check-raise a bully who will try to take the pot away from me if I blink (3) The chip position of my opponent is unsatisfactory; a nearly all-in opponent will surely call.

Let's talk about stack size, since it is vital to big-bet poker. The most important principle of exploiting stack size is "The threat is stronger than its execution." Not only does big-bet poker allow you to make a large bet; it also allows you to seriously threaten all an opponent's chips by the prospect of continued betting.

Suppose you and I are playing in a $5-$10-$25 blind game, and I have position on you. There is an unraised pot with a flop of 10-7-3 with no flush-draw. You bet a hundred dollars, and I raise you two hundred more. Let us look at the magnitude of decision you have, depending on the amount of money in front of you. (We will assume here that I have an equal amount or greater, so all your money is in play.)

(1) If you only have started with $300, the decision will be quite simple. There is only the $200 raise to think about. You have to assume that I probably have top pair or better, as a 9-8 is the only drawing hand an opponent might hold. With an A-10 or better, the call is automatic. With a hand such as K-10, Q-10 or J-10, for only a couple hundred bucks you will likely shut your eyes, put the money in, and pray. A lesser holding you will probably fold. It is not a difficult decision, not a lot of money is riding on it, and for a marginal hand like Q-10 there is not much difference in equity between folding and calling. (By "equity" I mean the average amount the hand figures to be worth if the situation came up repeatedly.)

(2) Suppose you have started the deal with $1,000. Now I have given you the added option of reraising all-in for $700 more, in addition to calling or folding. Also, if you decide to just call, what will you do on fourth street? Since to only call the raise and then check on the new card shows a certain amount of weakness, there is a good possibility I'll put you all-in on the next betting round. When the opponent has raised with money left to bet rather than all-in, the chance he has a big hand is greatly magnified. Obviously, my raise has forced you to think about a lot more than just the amount needed to call. All your

chips have been threatened, because they may all need to go into the pot to see the hand through.

(3) For our last scenario, let us assume your stack at the start of the hand was much more than $1,000. How big would it need to be so my $200 raise did not threaten it? If you call on the flop, there will be roughly $700 in the pot. A pot-size bet on each of the last two rounds ($700 on fourth street and $2,100 on fifth street) means the hand would cost about three grand in total. This assumes no raises, and only normal-size bets.

As you can see, my $200 bet has achieved an influence totally out of proportion to its size. The fact is any wager at big-bet poker gets an opponent thinking about how much it is going to cost him to see a hand through. The winning style of play is to use your wager as a threat to cost the opponent a lot of money, while not putting that much actually at risk yourself. The thought of any player facing a raise and caught without a big hand is usually, "Why get involved? I could get busted." This is what is meant when big-bet poker is called a game of intimidation.

Aggressiveness, bluffing, and bullying are key parts of a winning strategy. Once you are in combat, you need these tools to fight at full strength. But let me emphasize that even though you may have the ability to slug your way out of some tough corners, this is no reason to initially be in a corner. Get a good starting hand before doing battle. If that hand turns sour later on, only then do you try to fight for the pot anyway.

I think the biggest mistake many players make is to get involved without adequate values when an opponent raises the pot. Raises are supposed to be made on a hand such as A-Q, A-K, or a pair of nines through aces. Quite often, a raiser will not have this good a hand, but more than half the time he will. If your hand isn't this strong, you do not belong in the pot unless you are in position. Observing this simple standard will save you a lot of money. Let's look at a few simple situations and see whether you should get involved. Let us assume the game is a $5-$10-$25 blind pot-limit or no-limit game.

I. You hold A♠-J♠ under the gun. You call the quarter, and the player on your immediate left makes it $100. Everyone else folds. What do you do?

Answer: Fold. Your opponent has shown a good hand by raising a player who called in early position. His hand is superior to yours, and he has position on you. Someone who thinks this is a good place to call is using poor reasoning for a big-bet game. A faulty saying that could get you involved is, "You only get a certain number of good hands, so you've got to play them." This line of thought puts hands on a rigid scale of values. The correct thinking for any form of poker should be defining a good hand simply as one that figures to be the best on that deal. The betting has clearly shown your A♠-J♠ to flunk this test. Another lie that could cause trouble here is, "The pot odds favor a call." Those players who are primarily limit players get involved on far too many hands by chasing "pot odds." The key to big-bet play is to look at implied odds, what stands to be won or lost over and above the amount in the pot. We have already discussed how a player has to constantly think about his whole stack when there is a bet or raise. You must also think about it in deciding whether to call a raise before the flop. The right question to ask is, "If I call, who is more likely to get broke, him or me?" Any player who thinks he can take an A-J suited out-of-position and have the best of it against a raiser is a heck of a lot better player than I am—if he's right.

II. You hold 9♣-8♣ on the button. Three other players call a quarter, and so do you. The big blind, a solid player, raises $150 more, and two of the three players in front of you call. What should you do?

Answer: It depends on how deep the money is. Your position is the best possible, but you don't have much of a hand. A good rule to follow is the "Five and ten rule." When contemplating calling a raise because your position is good, you have a clear call if the amount is less than five percent of your stack, and a clear fold if it is more than ten percent. In between those numbers, use your judgment. Keep in mind that the raiser is your most likely target, so make sure he has plenty of money to be won, as well as watching your own ammunition supply. To get sufficient benefit out of good position, deep money is essential.

III. You hold 8-8 in the small blind. Several players call a quarter, and you call. The big blind raises $125 more, and two players call. What should you do?

Answer: Once again, it depends on how deep the money is. You should apply the rule of five and ten. Your position is fine for this type of hand. You can check the flop whether you hit or miss. The raiser will likely bet, putting the field in the middle. If you flop a set, you're well-placed to reap a good payoff. If the flop should be checked by all, the pot is yours for the taking any time a blank hits on fourth street. As your opponents see it, you are the player most likely to have checked a strong hand on the flop. Remember this important principle of big-bet hold'em: a drawing hand needs good position throughout the deal; a set needs good position only on the flop. Of course, being in position throughout the deal will help any hand, but a set can survive without it. Therefore, play connectors in a raised pot only in back position. Play an intermediate pair in most situations if the price is right in proportion to your stack.

IV. You hold A-A on the button. A player opens for $100 in early position and the field folds around to you. Do you play your hand straightforwardly and raise or try to trap your opponent with a call?

Answer: Contrary to what you may have read or been told, slowplaying a big pair can be a lucrative play at either pot-limit or no-limit hold'em. You have the nuts. It is essential that a big-bet poker player varies how he plays the nuts.

I believe slowplaying A-A or K-K before the flop is a fully acceptable play if three criteria are met: (a) You are heads-up (2) you have position on the opponent (3) the chip position is favorable for slowplaying a big pair. The first two criteria have been met in our problem. (Only the blinds are to be heard from.) What about the chips? What you want is the raiser to bet the flop, you raise him all-in, and he calls. If the money is shallow, it would be better to move all-in before the flop. If the money is deep, where you cannot move in on him at either pot-limit or no-limit without overbetting the pot, then he is often going to fold when he gets raised. If he does call a big bet you may well be beaten. We want to get him in a situation where his call after the flop will seem nearly automatic.

The layout described in the problem has $240 in the pot before the flop if the blinds fold. The perfect amount of money remaining would be around $700, which would be a $200 bet and a $500 raise. This is about three times the size of the pot. As a rule of thumb, slowplay a big pair before the flop only when the amount of money in play for your opponent is two to four times the pot size.

Remember that slowplaying a big pair against a raiser depends on him betting the flop. If you are up against a Timid Tim who probably wouldn't bet the flop heads-up unless he helps his hand, slowplaying will not work properly. All you would be doing is giving him a free shot to beat you. Use slowplaying only against reasonably aggressive players.

Let's talk a bit more on how you play the nuts. As mentioned before, it is necessary at big-bet poker to vary your play with big hands. An important element is chip position. Even if you are by both bankroll and temperament the kind of player who simply buys enough chips to cover all bets, you can't bet more than the opponent has in play. It is vital at big-bet poker that you be aware of the amount of money in front of each opponent. (This is why we prefer games that require all cash be converted to chips.)

Suppose you flop a set in a heads-up pot. Should you lead with it or check-raise? If the stack sizes allow you to move the opponent all-in by a check-raise without overbetting the pot, this is the better course of action. You win a bet from him when he is weak and couldn't call a bet from you, and he is likely to go with your check-raise if he has a decent hand like top pair. When the money is deeper, your best chance of doubling up is to bet the flop. If he raises, this may commit him to the pot for your reraise. If he calls, he may continue to call on fourth and fifth street, whereas the power play of a check-raise might have made him fold.

A lot of big-bet players have the bad habit of checking whenever they make a big hand. This works out badly for several reasons. First, it makes things too easy for an opponent to read you and thus do the right thing. Second, it creates a place in the betting where the opponent knows you have a big hand and has a chance to release his own hand and get away with a minor injury. If you simply keep charging the pot with bets on each street, there is no spot where he can be sure you are loaded for bear. Third, betting right out a good bit of the time with big hands gives more credibility to the many occasions where you will be betting and hoping the opponent will fold. Lastly, and perhaps most important, a check-raising style shows you are thinking about the game in the wrong way. Your goal in a no-limit game is to win all your opponent's money, not take little pecks. At hold'em, it is not easy to flop a hand big enough that you are hoping to back it with your whole stack. When you are fortunate enough to do so, think positively. Big hands are meant to play big pots. Train your sights on the opponent's entire stack. Play the hand the best way to get doubled up. It is faulty thinking to say to yourself, "I have three jacks, so I'm going to make sure I win a little something with them." With a big hand, aim at a big goal; doubling up. Remember that you are going to judge the session's success simply by how much money you won, not by the number of moderate-size pots you won.

Winning massive pots is your goal in a big-bet game. To be on the right side of these big swings you must choose your starting hands carefully, especially in raised pots. A good bit of the time, such a major confrontation will be between a big made hand and a big drawing hand, where anything can happen. But fairly often, the confrontation will be between two made hands. In such a matchup, the better hand has a huge advantage in a community-card game. You want to be on the right side of such situations.

When you look at both hands in a made-hand vs. made-hand all-in situation, the owner of the weaker hand will often moan, "I had to play." Much of the time this will be true. In other words, if a top player had held the weaker hand at the point the big money went into the pot, he would also have played and gotten broke. But quite often, the top player would not have been in before the flop. The way to avoid such traps is to not get involved in the first place! "What you sow is what you reap" applies especially well to hold'em. Solid play before the flop, particularly in raised pots, will keep you on the right side of these trap situations most of the time.

We mentioned the possibility of getting all-in with a drawing hand. Let's talk some more about this. At hold'em a made hand will usually be a favorite against a drawing hand. Nevertheless, to play the game in the best way, you mustn't be afraid of backing the right kind of draw with all your money. If you almost always have a big made hand when you bet strongly, the opponents will pick up on this and play accordingly. You will not get played with often enough on your big hands.

There is another reason to play a quality drawing hand strongly on the flop. Normally, a draw will be a solid contender for the pot only when there are two cards to come. A big draw at hold'em (as opposed to Omaha) will nearly always involve hitting a flush as one of the avenues for improvement. Of course, anyone can see when the fourth street card makes a possible flush. If you get only a portion of your stack into the pot on the flop, there is the strong possibility your opponent will make the correct play on fourth street. If you make your flush, he'll dump his hand. If you miss, he will charge you a very steep price to continue to draw at the last card. We'll talk more about this a little later.

Another reason to gun it out on the flop is that when a flush card hits, you may not know for sure where you stand. Suppose the flop is 10♣-7♥-5♥. With a top pair and flush-draw combination such as J♥-10♥, or a straight-and-flush draw such as 9♥-8♥, it is often better to move in on the flop instead of playing guessing games on fourth street. Besides, the opponent may well throw his hand away when you make a massive raise. Just be sure you make the same kind of big raise with this type of board when you have a set, instead of a modest-size amount begging for a call.

Just to keep your opponents off-balance, it is a good idea once in a while to smooth-call an opponent's bet on the flop—or even check and call—although there is a draw on the board. The best time to do this is with a flush-draw out there and no straight-draw, such as K♣-8♣-3♥. In such circumstances it is better to be slow-playing top set, or at least middle set, so if an opponent with a pocket pair hits trips on fourth street, it breaks him instead of you. We emphasize this play of slowplaying a set should not be done very often. Five or ten percent of the time is enough.

We have been talking about moving all-in with a drawing hand. Do you ever move in with no hand at all? Very rarely. It is always nice to have an escape hatch; a way to get lucky if the opponent calls. Here is an illustration. Suppose on the flop you move all-in $2,000 more on a $2,000 pot, have nothing, and get called. Your equity is zero. Now suppose that you have only the longshot of a belly straight draw. With two cards to come, you will make the straight about one time in six. This means your equity in the $6,000 pot is about a grand. You risked two grand when you bet, and wound up losing only half of it when you got called. This is a big improvement over zero equity. If you would have had as much as an open-end straight draw, your amount of risk would have been nothing, because you will win about a third of the time. Your equity would be $2,000, the amount you bet. This is why it pays to have outs when you move all-in.

Most people are aware of the need for outs when moving all-in at a big-bet game, but a lot of them extend the principle to situations where it is not an all-in bet. They refuse to make a bet or raise unless they have outs. Let us see why this is faulty thinking.

Suppose you start a no-limit deal with $1,500. An opponent bets a hundred, and you raise three hundred more. With hand number one, you have nothing. With hand number two, you have a straight draw. In both cases, the opponent plays back, moving you in for $1,100 more. Are you better off with outs? The answer is no. With hand number one, you fold and lose $400. With hand number two, you could either fold and lose the same $400, or you could call, and figure to lose slightly more than $400 on the average. (Your equity would be around a grand, and the hand costs $1,500.) In fact, the only way having outs would help is in the parlay of events where the opponent calls your $300 raise and then you make your hand.

Here is another situation. Suppose there is a pair on the board. Now a straight or flush draw is very much a double-edged sword. Do you wait for outs before bluffing a bet when the board is paired? If there is a pair on board and no straight or flush draw, would you refuse to ever bluff at the pot? For a flop like J-J-3 all offsuit, you will grow old waiting for a hand with outs so you can feel comfortable in launching a bluff. So make sure you have outs before moving in on someone with cards to come. But don't be afraid to sometimes make a bet or raise without any outs, if there is still money left to be bet. This can be a tool for seeming to threaten your opponent's entire stack without risking all of your own.

The main difference between pot-limit play and no-limit play is no-limit affords the possibility of getting all-in any time you want, whereas pot-limit does not. The desire to be all-in comes up most often on the flop betting round. For the big draw, there are two cards to come, which puts the hand in reasonable contention to win the pot against a made hand. If all the money goes in on the flop, the draw expects to be in reasonable shape. The draw does not want to get a quarter to half his stack in the pot, miss his hand on the fourth street card, and be set all-in. At hold'em, unless it is some kind of freak hand, the player's money is going to have to go in when he is a substantial underdog. And abandoning a big pot that might have been won is not a pleasant alternative to calling. Keep in mind that a big draw in hold'em is always going to include a flush-draw (something that is not necessarily true at Omaha), so the opponent is going to be aware of whether the drawing hand has likely connected or not, and act accordingly.

Here is an example of how a player facing a possible draw is going to behave. My co-author Stewart at pot-limit picked up A♥-K♠, raised preflop, and got called in several places. The flop came K♥-10♦-7♥. Stewart bet, an opponent raised, and the others folded. Stewart called the raise. (I probably would not have called in this type of situation, but Stew had played a lot of poker with this man, and was at the table to get information such as mood and mannerisms.) There was enough money left after the flop betting round for one full pot-size bet. The fourth street card was the 2♣. Now Stewart pounced and moved in with his stack. Despite the possibility that the opponent had a made hand—which in this case would be very likely better than Stew's—this all-in bet is superior to checking and allowing a drawing hand a free chance to beat you. It is vastly better than checking and then lamely calling an all-in bet. The point to calling on the flop was to take advantage of this type of situation where a drawing hand did not connect. Stewart's opponent called the fourth street all-in bet, evidently on a draw, but did not help his hand on the last card, and lost a big pot.

On this deal the made hand was greatly helped by catching a blank on fourth street, as any card six or higher would have created a potential straight on the board. A player out of position, as here, could easily have had a lot of nasty guesswork. If Stew would have had position, he could have seen his opponent's reaction to a possible straight or flush, and thus been more likely to do the right thing in that event. The player with a draw is at a big disadvantage out of position on fourth street.

Particularly at pot-limit hold'em, this use of position with a made hand to set the opponent all-in on fourth street when he blinks is an important tool. Sometimes you have to grit your teeth and do this on a modest holding, one that is likely beaten if you have been tricked by a strong made hand, but you cannot just blink back and let the money sit there, vulnerable to a drawout or hijacking. Most of the time an opponent who checks here is either drawing or on a shaky holding. After all, **you** may be drawing for all he knows, and most opponents with a strong made hand in this spot will move in, thinking, "The pot is big enough for me," instead of trapping.

The no-limit player with a big draw avoids this pot-limit dilemma by moving in with all his chips on the flop when there is already a large pot. Naturally, a player who moves all-in on the flop could easily have a made hand as well. The point is whenever you have a through ticket for all your money, it is undesirable to get caught out of position on fourth street on a big pot with money still left to bet.

Let us look at a typical hold'em betting situation and contrast how it would be handled in a pot-limit game as compared to a no-limit game. There are four players that see the flop. You are first and hold Q♠-J♠. The flop comes 10♠-9♠-3♣, a pleasant sight, giving you a straight-flush draw with two overcards. You want to make a play for the pot and are willing to back your hand with your entire stack if need be. Let us assume there is a hundred dollars in the pot and each player has a grand in front of him.

The game plan of the no-limit player might well be to check this hand and go for a check-raise. If someone bets the size of the pot, he can raise the person all-in. He would be calling the $100 (making the pot now $300) and raising $900 more all-in. (The no-limit player could adopt this same game plan if he had flopped a concealed set; moving in doesn't necessarily show a draw.)

I do not like going for a check-raise in this spot if the game is pot-limit instead of no-limit. If an opponent called your check-raise, this would create a $900 pot with $600 left to bet, and you would be out of position on the critical betting round. The opponent may well be able to set you all-in if you miss your draw and get away from his hand if you connect. It is the superior play to simply bet the flop. If the opponent calls, you have flexibility in how to handle the fourth street betting, because there is only $300 in the pot. Your drawing hand will have the handy leverage of money left to bet on the end if there is a bet and call on fourth street, increasing your equity in the pot. If the opponent chooses to raise you on the flop, you come back over the top and set him all-in. His position would now be worthless and you would have two cards to come if he called, giving you a fine chance to make your draw.

We know that drawing hands are much better if we have position on the hand. These examples of distress for a drawing hand on fourth street when being unable to get all-in on the flop show that at pot-limit play the suffering for positional inferiority is even greater than at no-limit. Keep this fact in mind for preflop hand selection and take special care to avoid building an out-of-position drawing hand at pot-limit.

A situation where you might use the no-limit structure's opportunity of getting all-in any time you want is with a preflop raise. If a pot-size raise would be such a large hunk of your stack that you are committed to go all the way with your hand (about forty percent of your stack on the initial raise) it is better to simply open the pot by going all-in. This forces an opponent who calls to make the same commitment to the pot as you. This scenario comes up much more often in tournament play than money games.

No-limit play differs from pot-limit play by allowing you to overbet the amount in the pot. We have seen that the main way to take advantage of this is to move all-in at the appropriate moment. There are some other situations aside from all-in betting when you may want to overbet the pot size. The first one is up front in a blind when making a preflop raise. To have the opposition fold is a good result, and if an opponent wishes to play out a pot with position on us he should be made to pay substantially for the privilege. A typical up-front raise is to overbet the pot by around fifty percent, and to raise an amount twice the pot size is not that uncommon.

The second use is when you want to diagram a specific holding that seems improbable, such as completing a backdoor flush on the end. The overbet leaves no doubt as to what is implied, and would be used whether bluffing or not.

The third use is to give the opponent a bad price on a draw. When the board is cluttered on fourth street with a lot of possible straight-draws and maybe a double flush-draw, it is unpleasant for the made hand on the last card. An all-in bet may be too large a commitment, but it may be right to try and remove the opponent by an overbet. Keep in mind that the drawing hand has a lot of leverage because of the potential bet on the end, increasing his implied odds.

The fourth use is for psychological reasons. An overbet is not necessarily a sign of strength. More often, it is a sign that the bettor is worried about something and does not want to be called. sometimes, an overbet will make the opponent think you are bluffing. The macho-man falls for this ploy easily; the tightwad does not. Know your opponent.

In reading this chapter on no-limit and pot-limit hold'em, the thing that should impress you the most is the enormous number of weapons a good player has working for him to achieve an advantage. The point is a good player's overlay at pot-limit and no-limit is much greater than at limit play because he has far more tools available. Although the fluctuation on a given hand may be greater, the longterm swings usually turn out to be less.

17-BIG-BET HOLD'EM QUIZ
by Bob Ciaffone

Problems one through eight have their setting in money-game play; problems nine through twelve are taken from tournament play. The first six problems can be considered to be in a pot-limit game, although the answer would be the same at no-limit. The final six problems are in a no-limit format. Assume unless otherwise stated that the game is nine-handed, using blinds of $15 and $25, with everybody in the game having at least a couple of grand in chips. Pay close attention to the size of your stack, as in this form of competition the amount of money involved is even more important.

(1) You are in the blind with 9♠-9♣. Everyone folds around to the button, who opens the pot for $100. The little blind folds, and it's up to you. What is your action?

Answer —   raise (10)   call (7)   fold (0)

Explanation — There is no way to know if 9♠-9♣ is the best hand. It is clearly too good a hand to fold when the button raises, as he may be simply trying to pick up the blind money on a very modest holding. My advice against most players is you should reraise. If he calls, bet half a grand on the flop no matter what comes. The chances are very good that he won't be able to stand the heat. But use your head. Don't make this play against a calling station or someone who likes to smooth-call a reraise when holding a big pair. As you can see, I have an aversion to calling a decent-size raise heads-up out-of-position when holding an intermediate strength pocket pair. The odds are over 7-1 against flopping a set, and it's often difficult to double through the opponent from in front of him when you do hit trips. If you flop an overpair, it is still hard to know where you stand. My advice is to take a firm position on the hand before the flop. If your opponent is a solid player who raised in early position, then fold. If you think the opponent may lack solid values for his raise, then play back at him. But avoid simply calling when you are heads-up out-of-position with this type of hand.

(2) You pick up pocket aces in middle position. The player under-the-gun opens for a raise, the next couple of opponents fold, and it's up to you. Do you figure to get a better result by reraising or smooth-calling?

Answer —   raise (10)   call (5)   fold (-100)

Explanation — If you simply call, your position will be abysmal if other players enter the pot behind you. A bet by the raiser will run you into a lot of trouble if those aces get out-flopped. The better play is to reraise before the flop. There is a decent chance of getting called, or even played back at. After all, an early position raiser figures to have a good hand.

I remember a deal many years ago where this exact situation arose. I smooth-called with the aces against an under-the-gun raise by Robert Turner. Everyone else folded. The flop came ace-rag-rag. I won the pot, of course, but made nary a penny after the flop. As it turned out, my opponent held pocket kings. He was annoyed at that ace coming on the flop—until I showed him my hand. A reraise before the flop would have won me a big pot, perhaps even a double-up. Until this deal, I didn't fully realize how bad a play using aces to smooth-call an early-position raiser was.

(3) You pick up pocket queens in middle position and open for a raise to $100. Only the player on your left and the player on the button call. The flop comes K♦-8♦-2♣. Do you check or bet?

Answer —   Check (10)   bet (7)

Explanation — With this texture flop you should vary your game by sometimes betting and other times checking. Checking shouldn't mean the opponents have a green light to steal. For example, if I had raised with A-K, I would vary my action with this type of flop, perhaps betting about two-thirds of the time. If I check the flop because my hand is less than top pair, I would be more likely to hold Q-Q or J-J than A-Q or A-J. Generally, it is better to bet when you do not have even a pair to show down, and to check when you have a little something. I would normally check a pair of queens here. Not many free cards are going to beat me. If someone bets, there is a good chance I'll fold. If the opponents both check the flop, it will look as if the coast is clear for me to bet on fourth street.

(4) You pick up A♣-9♣ in late position. The player on your immediate right opens the pot for $100. What do you do?

Answer —   fold (10)   raise (5)   call (0)

Explanation — Your position relative to the raiser is the worst possible. An ace suited with a middle-sized or low card is not a strong hand. It is basically a drawing hand requiring very favorable position to playing in a raised pot. You have a clear fold. A reraise is preferable to a call.

 (5) You are in the big blind in a $5-$10 game looking at a pair of deuces in a six-handed unraised pot. The flop comes 8♦-5♥-2♠, giving you bottom set. The person who had the little blind leads at the pot for $60; you just call. Gary, a sound player in middle position who had been the second person to enter the pot, raises to a total of $170. The rest of the field and the original bettor all fold. You and Gary each have about a grand left. What do you do?

Answer —   fold (10)   call (3)   raise (0)

Explanation — You must think about what the opponent is likely to hold. With an overpair of jacks through aces, it seems probable that he would have raised a preflop, as a player had opened the pot ahead of him. With a pair of nines or tens, if he did not raise preflop, he would likely have made a larger raise in this spot than $110 more with a $240 pot, as he'd want to shut you out. Two pair such as eights and fives looks remote. I decided that my opponent had probably flopped a set, and mucked my three deuces. After the session, I told Gary about my laydown, and he said I had done the wrong thing. Gary then kind of dropped out of sight for quite a while. About five years later I ran into him at a poker tournament. He said, "Hello, remember me?" and I replied that I did. He continued, "There is something I've been meaning to tell you for a long time. Remember that deal up at The Lake where you folded trips against me? I didn't tell you the truth afterwards. I had flopped top set and you made a good laydown." I smiled, and thanked him for being honest with me. You don't have to get broke every time you flop a set and it is no good.

(6) You pick up J♥-10♥ in the big blind. Three people call a quarter and the button raises to $125 straight. The little blind folds; what do you do?

Answer—fold (10)   Call (3)   Raise (1)

Explanation: Your position will be bad throughout the deal, but especially so on the flop betting round, where a bet by the preflop raiser would come through you with the field yet to act. You have a reasonable hand, but the jack-ten suited is basically a drawing hand. A drawing hand needs good position, particularly at pot-limit.

(7) You pick up A♠-K♠ in late position and open for a raise to $100 straight. The big blind is the only caller. He is a very aggressive and tricky player named Hurley. The flop comes nice for you; A♦-9♥-3♠. You have top pair with top kicker. Hurley checks and you bet $200. He calls. The next card is an innocuous 8♥. He checks, you bet $400, and he calls again. The last card is the 2♣. To your surprise, the opponent now springs to life with an all-in bet of $1,500, slightly more than the pot size of $1,415. Obviously, he is either bluffing or can easily beat one pair. What should you do?

Answer —   fold (10)   call (0)

Explanation — Your opponent almost surely has a hand that is better than yours. The flop did not offer any drawing prospects. By his call on the flop and on fourth street, your opponent showed that he had made a hand. He has little need to bluff. If his hand were something like A-Q or A-J, it would be natural for him to check after the final card, and certainly not to make a big bet. Your hand belongs in the muck. I folded this hand, and my opponent told me later that he had flopped a set of nines. There are two lessons to be learned here. The first is that an opponent with a made hand is not likely to try and win the pot by representing a bigger hand than actually held. The normal action is to simply show it down and hope for the best. The second is when an opponent whose betting late in a hand is inconsistent with his betting early in a hand, the later information is likely to be the truth.

(8) You hold A♥-10♥. The flop comes 10♦-7♦-3♥. Three of you stayed for the flop in an unraised pot, so there is about a hundred dollars in the pot. The first player bets $100, the second player folds, and you call. On fourth street comes the 2♥, which makes you a four-flush. Your opponent bets $250. You call, making $800 now in the pot. The last card is the pleasant J♥, giving you the nut flush. Your opponent checks. How much do you bet?

Answer — $1000 (10) $800 (8) $500 (5)

Explanation — I think in these situations the best thing to do is overbet the pot. An even grand looks like a good figure. When a backdoor flush gets completed on the last card, and you either have the flush, or have nothing and wish to bluff, the right thing to do is overbet the pot. This makes it crystal clear that you are representing a flush, and it shouldn't make any difference to the opponent whether he has one pair, two pair, a set, or even a straight. Either you have him beaten by holding a flush, or you busted out and are bluffing. At least there is no misunderstanding about what you are representing.

(9) It is early in the second day of the 1987 World Championship. You and Jay Heimowitz, a wily and aggressive veteran from New York, are tournament co-leaders at this point, each with just over a hundred thousand dollars in chips. As fate would have it, you're at the same table. Jay is in the big blind and you are on the button. The hand you are dealt is a rare and pretty sight; a pair of aces. Everyone folds and you make a small raise. Jay is your only caller. There is about eight grand in the pot. The flop comes 10♦-6♥-4♠. Jay checks. How do you play the hand?

Answer —   check (10)   bet (6)

Explanation — In a tournament, when you have a big stack of chips, you should avoid major confrontations with another big stack. How far out of your way you should go is a course a matter of debate. I will say this; if you get all-in with this kind of flop against Jay Heimowitz for a hundred grand apiece when there was only eight thousand in the pot, those aces will not be the best hand. My plan was to make some money in the likely event my aces were still boss, and not get broke if they weren't. I checked on the flop. On fourth street Jay bet $6,000 and I just called. On the end Jay bet $12,000 and I simply called again. His hand was a pair of queens. As there were small cards on the board, I won the pot, picking up just over twenty grand from a dangerous opponent. Note that the way this hand was played, I was never in danger of getting broke or bluffed. If I had bet on the flop and continued betting, I probably would have made about the same amount of money, because he likely would have called both on the flop and fourth street, and released the hand on the end. Of course, aces are the best starting hand to play in the fashion I described, as the free card you give will not be an overcard.

(10) This hand is from the 1982 World Championship. You are in the big blind and have A♣-Q♥. Three-time World Champion

Johnny Moss opens under the gun for $700 and Sam Moon calls. Since it was only $500 more to you, you decide to call. The flop comes Q♠-7♥-2♥, giving you top pair with an ace kicker. You lead at the pot for $1,000, Moss calls, and Moon folds. The next card is the 3♥, making a three-flush on board. You lead at the pot again, this time for $4,000, and Moss calls. The last card is the 6♠, a blank. John has about another nine grand in front of him (you have bit more than that). What does Moss hold, and should you check or put him all-in?

Answer —   check (10)   bet (5)

Explanation — Moss's hand is almost certainly a big pair, either aces or kings, likely with a heart that could have made a flush on the last card. You obviously do not hold the winning hand, so if you bet, it would be a bluff. Whether to bluff is a difficult question. I decided it was not good poker to try and run a World Champion off a big pair, and checked the hand. Moss checked it back and showed down two red kings. Would he have called $9,000 bet on the end? I asked him that question at dinner that night. His reply was an honest-sounding "I don't know." Then he added, "Probably, but I wouldn't have liked it." My feeling to this day has been that I did the right thing, but of course there is no way to know for sure. My opinion is you should save your bluffs for situations where you think the opponent is weak, and not be trying to induce a big laydown.

(11) You are playing in the 1982 World Championship. It is the start of the third day, and you have about $22,000 in chips, which is a short stack for this late in the tournament. On your immediate right is Jack Straus, a highly aggressive player, and the eventual winner of the event. Jack has over quarter of a million in front of him, allowing his throttle to go full out. You are in the big blind and pick up A♣-8♥. The structure is $100 ante, $200 and $400 blind, so there is about $1,400 in the pot to start. Everybody folds around to Jack, who opens for a $4,000 bet. What do you do?

Answer —   raise (10)   fold (2)   call (1)

Explanation — Raise him all your money. Jack does not need to have anything in this spot. He would likely raise on any two cards rather than just calling the blind or throwing his hand away. Although you don't have any great shakes of a hand for an ordinary situation, it is fine holding for your present circumstance. Essentially, you are heads-up against a random hand and hold an ace, which is a through ticket for a short stack. It is clearly correct to raise all your money rather than a portion, because you are so committed to the pot that you would have to call a reraise anyway. On the actual deal Straus held K♣–9♣, which is a far stronger hand than average. Even so, he decided to fold. As it happens, a king was coming on the flop, and you would have lost the pot had you not run him out. (This was back in the days when rabbit-hunting was allowed in tournaments.)

(12) In this problem you are asked to play detective. Where did I go wrong? I was at the final table at the 1987 World Championship $10,000 buy-in event. There were three players remaining to fight it out for the title; myself, Frank Henderson, and Johnny Chan. I was the chip-leader with $665,000, Chan had $525,000, and Henderson the remainder, about a quarter million. The structure was now a $2,000 ante and blinds of $10,000 and $20,000. I was in the big blind and picked up A♦-4♦. John called on the button and Frank also called. I raised $85,000 more, and John surprised me by calling the raise. The flop came K♣-J♠-4♣, giving me only bottom pair. I made a sort of semi-bluff by betting $185,000. Chan moved all-in on me by making a $240,000 raise with the quickness of a pouncing tiger. I thought a long time. It seemed remote that he would be on a draw, but it certainly look like an ace or four would win the pot for me, and make me a huge favorite to become the World Champion. Since I was almost getting the right odds, and would still be in the hunt if I lost the pot, I called the raise. We faced our hands, and John showed a K♥-Q♠. I failed to draw out,

and became the first player in poker history to lose a pot with over a million dollars in it. A short while later, I lost another pot and finished in third place. Johnny Chan went on to become the 1987 World Champion. Did I make a mistake, and if so, where was it?

Answer—betting the flop (10) calling the raise (5) preflop raise(1)

Explanation — I think my pre-flop raise was quite reasonable, as you can't sit still in your chair at the price of $36,000 every three deals. My call on the end, though slightly unsound mathematically on the actual hands, was also reasonable. There was a remote chance my opponent was drawing, and there was the opportunity to get out of having to play heads-up against possibly the world's best no-limit player if I got lucky and drew out. But my bet on the flop cannot be justified. What kind of hand limps in and then calls $85,000 more? I have played a lot of poker with John, and I feel sure he would have reraised me playing threehanded if he had a pocket pair. So he was very likely to have big cards that fit the flop of K-J-4. I should have checked that flop. I played my best poker in that event to get as far as I did, but it only takes one mistake to cost you a tournament—and the title of World Champion. Even so, my experiences at the final table were the greatest thrill in my life.

Scoring: 120 = perfect
                      110-118 = very strong
                      100-109 = good player
                        90-99 = not bad
                        80-89 = need more study
              less than 80 = bring lots of money

18 - POT LIMIT OMAHA
"Never Call Solely To Make A Hand Which May Be A Loser"

by Stewart Reuben

This book assumes you have read Bob's comprehensive work "Omaha Holdem Poker." Not to have done so is a crime against nature. This chapter simply expands some concepts.

Omaha is a very peculiar game, in that before the flop, you really want everybody to pass. Within reason, whatever the quality of your opponent's hand, he will almost certainly have a fair chance of beating you. Thus, the very real question. Why raise before the flop?

A-A-J-10 double-suited or A-A-K-K double-suited are the best hands before the flop. People have asked me, "Which do you prefer?" Frank Thompson, when I answered, "What does it matter?," opined, "Because it decides how you play after the flop." Another told me, in his experience, A-A-J-10 double-suited won more money. In my experience, I don't have the choice. In fact I have only once had A-A-K-K double suited; it is 50,000-1 against. This is not much more likely than a pat straight flush in five cards. Whatever, the hand isn't a 3-2 favorite against 8-7-6-5 double-suited before the flop. If you "know" your opponent has aces, this is the best type of hand to outdraw him. If you are late to speak and several people are already in the pot, then a raise isn't going to make a substantial number fold. Thus the only reason to raise with aces is to augment the pot when you can't have the worst of it. If, by so doing, you reveal half your hand, this is dangerous. Thus, you must raise with a variety of hands. The view has been expressed that a good player should wait to escalate the pot size until after the flop, when he may have made a more durable hand. But you **must** sometimes raise preflop, to discourage people from limping in with the certainty they will not have to face a raise. When somebody has raised immediately in front of you, then a reraise with aces is excellent. Weaker hands are likely to be driven out, because now they are getting less than 2-1 for their money.

In poker, whenever you raise before your hand is made, you are increasing the size of the stakes. Naturally, this violently increases your pluses and minuses. The standard deviation of your profit-loss account is a much larger number. However, although the standard deviation will be higher, it should not be proportionately as large as the increase in total win. You are choosing the battlefield when you have a good hand. This strategy cannot be considered when your funds are too low to permit it. When playing on limited resources, there is much more to be said for keeping the size of the pot down.

Consider the following preflop hand against Mansour Matloubi (the 1990 Hold'em World Champion) and Eddie, two ultra-aggressive players. Mansour had put up the $50 blind. On the button I made it the maximum $200. Now Eddie called, making the pot $550, and raised the whole amount. Mansour now faced a bet of $700 to win $1100. He called. It was $550 to me and I raised the maximum with A♣-A♠-10♣-9♠. Although this is not the best conceivable attacking hand, it is the best defense, as it is impossible to construct a hand which wouldn't like some of mine for draws. Eddie called the $2350 and raised all-in a further $1000, and Mansour called the $3350. Naturally I called the $1000, not being allowed to use the under-raise to take further action. The pot stood at $12,400. Note; after the pot, we discussed the matter and all three of us were convinced Eddie and I both had aces. The flop was K♦-8♥-4♥. Mansour checked. Although this flop is totally irrelevant to me, it is also one of the least dangerous. Mansour cannot be certain of having the best flush draw against me. It is unlikely he has stood all this action with 8-8, 4-4 or K-4 in his hand. Thus the only real dangers are K-K, K-Q-J-8 or 8-7-6-4. With a fine drawing hand such as 8-7♥-6♥-5, it would be better to come out betting. Although odds-on versus dry aces, it's less than a 2-1 favorite. So he should bet, hoping for a pass. I bet $12,000 and Mansour raised the final $2000, which I gloomily called. The last cards were the J♠ and 7♦, giving me the nut straight with 10-9.

Mansour's actual holding was K♥-K♣-J♥-2♦. Eddie indeed did have the other two aces. Thus my only win was to hit a backdoor straight with no heart flush coming up. This is about 2% probability. What is even sadder for Mansour is that Eddie only had the bare A♥, so that a heart flush would have given him the whole pot. To crown my victory, Eddie told me that had a queen popped up on the last card, he would have split his part of the pot with me, as he too had an A-10 combination.

Although this is the most monstrous, brutal, biggest out-draw I have ever pulled off, I am still convinced Mansour should have passed before the flop. His probability of winning when holding kings under aces does not justify the outlay.

I store the memory of these monstrous out-draws that I have pulled. Then, when somebody destroys me in a similar manner, I lie back and bask in the warm glow of a pot long since gone. This helps me avoid going on tilt.

Understandably, you may wonder what is the biggest conceivable out-draw in a reasonable poker pot. Consider the following scenario in a seven-stud game: Anna (A♣ A) A 5♣. George (? ?) 9 9. Olaf (? ?) A. The game is three-handed and Olaf passed on the first betting round. On fourth street the remaining two players go all-in. It now turns out George has four 9's. The only way for Anna to win is to hit 4♣ 3♣ 2♣. The probability of this is: (3 x 2 x 1) / (43 x 42 x 41), which is 0.0081%, about 12,340 to 1. Now that's what I call a juicy out-draw!

Some beginners ask, "Since any flop may come up, what makes one holding superior to another before the flop?" e.g. What's so terrible about Q-7-3-2 offsuit? What sort of flop are you hoping to hit? Q-Q-7 or 7-7-7 or 5-4-A are examples. But who is going to contest a big pot with you if such a miracle flop comes? On Q-Q-7, only 7-7 or a Queen with sidecards bigger than your 7, so that you may end up losing, having flopped the nuts. Of course, you are going to win with a flop of 7-7-7, but it will only be a small pot. You may win on 5-4-A, but no improving card such as a pair, flush, or potentially bigger straight card as an 8, 7, 6, 3 or 2 will leave you with a certainty.

In poker, when determining the odds, it is not only what you will win if you make your hand, but also the potential for winning fresh money once you have done so, and the likelihood of losing more.

In addition, a good hand before the flop has a better chance of success. If you are double-suited, you have a much better chance of hitting a flush. Four cards in sequence have a vastly greater number of ways to make a straight than just two cards in sequence. If you start with a pair, then at least you have that to show down at the end of the hand.

If you play K-9-6-6, you are obviously hoping to hit a 6. Calling breaks our homily at the beginning of the chapter. It is **impossible** to hit a 6 without there being either higher cards or a straight on the table. Whether the flop is 6-3-2 or 8-6-2, there is no security. The hand is garbage. The higher your pair is, the fewer overcards are possible and the more likely undercards will turn up.

PLAY AFTER THE FLOP

Let's consider our play against various flops when we hold Q♥-9♣-8♥-7♦. Nothing much, but it was cheap to come in and we have good position.

(1) Flop 10♥-5♥-2♣. Under no circumstances call any bet with this hand. How can we put it? If you intend to call, rather send us the money; we have better use for it. You are calling to make a hand which may be beaten in the making, a cardinal sin. If everybody has checked to you, by all means bet if you want to. Then switch to passive no matter what later transpires in the pot. It is unwise to carry bluffs through to the bitter end in Omaha.

(2) Flop 10♥-6♥-2♣. This is more like it. Now you have seven nut outs; two 9's, three 8's and two 7's. A call is in order, facing one bet. A bet if everybody has checked, still a bluff, is much better than before. The problem now comes when an opponent check-raises. You must pass, and your own action has lost you the chance of an out-draw.

(3) Flop 10♥-6♥-5♣. Now you have risen to ten nut outs and can
genuinely enter into the fray. If there has been a bet and two
callers before you, this hand should probably still be junked.
One player may have trips and another the nut flush draw. You
must not only improve, but also have the hand stand up. As like
as not somebody has some of your straightening cards as well.

THE OUTS

The drawing cards with which a player can make the
winning hand are known as the outs. It takes 13 of these to be a
favorite to improve with two cards to come. However, the opponent
may make a full house in the meantime. Thus a draw needs at least
18 outs against trips to become the favorite.

Let us consider some Omaha hands against the action flop
of J♥-10♥-4♠. We assume we are up against trips when drawing.
It has been assumed that if you hit the nut flush, no opponent will
have a straight flush.

Hand	# of outs	# of nut outs	# of killer nuts
(1) A♥-K♠-Q♠-9♥	21	21	0
(2) K♥-Q♥-9♠-8♠	24	12	2
(3) A♥-A♠-K♥-Q♠	18	18	3
(4) A♣-K♣-Q♦-9♦	16	11	0
(5) K♣-Q♣-9♦-8♦	20	10	0
(6) A♥-A♠-K♠-2♥	13	11	0
(7) Q♥-9♠-8♣-6♣	17	5	0
(8) Q♥-10♠-10♣-9♥	21	6	3
(9) J♠-J♦-5♠-3♣	30 cards can come which might beat you.		

I don't think I have ever had Number 2, but I still wouldn't
want to fall in love with it for my entire bankroll. Well, that's true
of any hand.

Take a look at what misery might await Number 7. Imagine the disaster if you are up against Number 2. Now the only way you can win money is with a blank 6; or to hope for a split. Your Q-9-8-6 is an abomination, despite an amazing 17 outs.

Number 8 is a peculiar hand; apart from the nuts, you don't know what you want to hit, and you may be winning. I want to go all-in heads-up with this. Otherwise, I'll only get a headache trying to figure out what's happening. Thus the ultimate premium hand is hand number one with 21 outs. What if it is up against K♥-Q♥-J♣-J♠? Well, now you have 19 outs, of which 6 split the pot. Consider this to be 16 and the hand is still even money.

Hands 2, 3, 6 and 8 all hold out the possibility of killer cards. These are straight flushes, four of a kind, or over-trips, which may leave your opponent with at best one out.

Number 3 has an added attraction. If you are up against an opponent holding J-10, then pairing a four will win you the pot.

The ultimate drawing hand is different. Flop A♥-5♣-4♣. You hold A♣-A♠-6♣-7♥. Now you have 21 outs on the flop, and 23 with a card to come if fourth street is a blank. This assumes your opponent holds 3 2 ? ? The best defense is 7♣-6♥-3♣-2♣, and even then you are a 7-3 favorite. This is because all your nuts are killers. Interestingly enough, 7♣-6♥-3♣-2♣ is favorite against any hand which includes only the straight; yes, even A-A-3-2.

When you first play Omaha, you should train yourself to know at a glance how many possible outs there are on the flop and how many you hold, if drawing.

Several of the hands shown hold another attraction; the presence of a back-door flush draw. This comes up only 3% but that is not to be sniffed at. Hand 3 provides the best example. Fourth street J♥ 10♥ 4♠ 2♠. Now you hold 22 nut outs (assuming the 6♠, 5♠, or 3♠ doesn't give your opponent a straight flush) and are a favorite against nut trips with no defense.

It is rare to have a drawing hand which is a favorite against trips, even with two cards to come. And then, it is difficult to be more than a 5-4 favorite. The great attraction is the "macho" (even for a woman) one of dumping your money into the pot without a made hand.

When heading for an all-in coup against the nut trips, you may be able to shade the odds in your favor. The pot stands at $1K. He bets $1K, you raise $3K, and now he raises $9K with $10K left. You are certain you are up against trips. Then it is best to call. If an open pair emerges, you can pass. If a blank hits the table, you still have pot odds. If your hand comes up, he must call. There is $37K in the middle, and thus he is getting 3.7 to 1 for his money. The only possible loss is where the river would have brought you a killer card when an open pair breaks out on fourth street.

Sometimes you must be careful not to second-guess yourself. I had A♠-Q♥-10♣-4♣ with a flop of A♥-10♥-9♣. This flop is extremely explosive; there are more drawing possibilities than you can shake a deck at. There had been little action before the flop, and pretty soon the hand was down to two of us, with $3K in the middle. Fourth street brought (A♥-10♥-9♣) 3♠. I checked, and he bet $3K with only $1K left, exuding power. I just called, reasoning that I would pass if a heart came on the river and he bet. Either he had me beaten or he was on an even-money draw. The last card was (A♥-10♥-9♣-3♠) 4♠. I checked, he bet $1K all-in, and I called. He proved to hold Q♣-J♠-8♥-7♦, a 20-card draw. Of course, he could and should have saved the last bet, but I might conceivably have been on a draw as well. I should have set him in on fourth street. My reasoning was a **major** mistake. Had a non-straightening heart been delivered at the river, I would have thrown away $10K.

FLOPPING THE NUTS

For example, a flop of 10♣-7♣-6♦. You bet holding 9-8 for the straight (nothing extra) and one person calls. Now an open pair, club, 9, or 8 leaves you totally vulnerable. It is often best to pass, holding neither defense nor improvers, if bet at or raised. The 10♣-9♠-6♣ is still worse. Now a pair, club, K, Q, J, 8 or 7 can all do you in. Your hand is unplayable against a raise.

The true value of your flopped nuts, if a straight or full house, lies in the number of freeroll outs you have if an opponent has flopped the same hand.

Flop 10-10-7 and you hold A-K-10-7 is magnificent. Should he hold 10-7-6-5, then you are on a freeroll of 6 cards, twice over. This is a healthy 27% advantage with no risk. Many players when they flop such a hand want to give a free card and check it, even in last position. This can be a good way to win small. You may be called on the river if somebody makes a straight, or someone may try to steal the pot. To win big, you need an opponent with 10-7 or 7-7 or A-10. There is another disadvantage in the slowplay; if a picture turns up, you may have been outdrawn. This is more pronounced holding 3-2 with a flop of 3-3-2. Any card will give a possibly superior full house. The pot needs winning immediately.

PLAY WHEN THERE IS AN OPEN PAIR

If you don't have trips, then usually you can forget taking any action in such pots if there are several players still in. Somebody is lurking. Playing the trips or full house is more complex.

Holding 9-9 with a flop of 9-7-7, It is usually best to bet. You don't want to give a free card to an overpair, and somebody with a 7 will usually call. If somebody has already acted, it is okay to slowplay your monster, or to raise. The holding of 9-7 isn't that unusual, and action from A-7 is common. If a third 7 turns up later, forget the pot, and hope he will give you a free card to see the gorgeous case 9.

If you hold a 7 with this flop, again it is usually best to bet. Then, when somebody calls or raises, you know much more about what is going on. I play in a game where if everybody shows weakness, then somebody may well try to snatch the pot— especially me. With a 7 you do not want to face the additional headache of a possible bluff. If you are in a tight game, then a hand such as 7-6-5-4 can be checked to the river, in the hope of winning the unbet pot. Unfortunately, you will probably be outdrawn.

Most people check 7-7 (quad sevens) to the end. This is because the hand is so strong it is hard to get action on it. If fourth street brings (9-7-7) J, it is often worth a bet. Somebody may be out there with 9-9 or J-J, and sometimes 10-8 calls. Checking to the river often picks up small sums, but seldom lumps. If I have J-J and the pot has been checked, now I bet, and somebody else wants to take heavy action, I become deeply suspicious. If it has been bet early on I am much more likely to fall into the trap.

MULTIHANDED ACTION ON THE FLOP

You have 9-7. The flop is 9-7-7,and you bet and get two callers. Forget it. One has 9-9. This is the advantage of leading out, You can read your opponents' cards with X-ray vision; a bluff-call is meaningless. The flop is 9-9-7 and you hold 7-7. You bet, the next raises, and another reraises. Chuck this away. Both have a 9, and one may well have 9-7, the cards being close together. Even if not, the probability of your being outdrawn is very high.

When the flop is J-J-3 and you hold 3-3, the situation is more interesting. If there has been no action before the flop, then the possibility that one holds J-3 is about 14%. With substantial action before the flop, this is less likely. Let us imagine you holding A-K-3-3 double-suited and there has been one raise before the flop. You lead out, the next player raises, and a third calls. If there is a great deal of money left, your hand belongs in the trash. All the initiative lies with your opponents on the next two cards. However, if you can get the pot all-in now, it is well worth considering. You are favorite against two opponents, each with a jack and three random cards, as part of the time they are matching one or more of their cards. Your edge is tiny, and a discreet pass may be sounder. (Where the flop is A-A-7, then 7-7 should **always** be given up against two opponents. An A-7 is quite feasible because they may be in the same suit.) Returning to J-J-3, if you hold a J facing a bet, look around for an A. An A-J may be winning. The problem with raising and facing two opponents is that you are an underdog to improve. Thus, if you hold A-J-8-7 and somebody has bet, it is usually correct just to call. If a third player raises, you can pass.

Although you have nine outs, one opponent is probably matching one of these. Against only one player, matters are different. Holding A♥-J♣-8♥-7♣ with a flop of J♥-J♠-3♥, your flush-draw may be valuable, since an enemy full house is less likely.

The holding J-10♣-9♣-7 with a flop of 7-7♣-6♣ is interesting. This is worth couping along. The 8♣ gives you an ultra-monster. You may outdraw A-7 with a club, pair or straight. Beware a hand such as Q-Q-10-7. Now you have only six improving cards. This is only worth a bet, hoping to win unopposed. A call is out of the question unless you suspect a bluff. A-Q-Q-7 is more difficult. Against one flat bet you may be winning.

ILL-COORDINATED FLOPS

For example, the flop is K-7-2 where you hold J-8-7-7. You bet under the gun and are raised. He probably doesn't have trip kings because most people slowplay such monsters, holding position. This is the only advantage of kings over aces. With the former, all that can happen to you is an ace or quads arriving. Had the flop been A-7-2 and you held A-A-9-8, then a 5, 4, or 3 could come to spell ruination.

Holding A-Q-2-2 where the flop is K-7-2, I have played in some games where I am happy to go all-in, and others where I've thrown this away in response to a frown from one of the players. The flop of K-10-2 interests me more in this situation. Then I have five nut outs, and my opponent may be on a drawing hand.

Holding K-7, you are out on your own if there is action. Holding 7-2 is simple. Pass if somebody bets but bet yourself if in late position. A-Q is of similar merit; you are often winning this pot shorthanded against checkers.

X-RAY VISION

The flop is 9-8-2 and you hold K-Q-J-10. There is a bet and a call. You have 13 nut outs and position; a call is in order.

Fourth street is (9-8-2) 3. Again there is a bet and call. It is very likely the middle player has at worst J-10. This would reduce you to seven splits and four wins. A pass is in order, especially if the 3 makes a potential flush which you don't hold.

Even on fourth street, the drawing hand can be a favorite against two opponents with made hands. Look at this layout where the board is 10♦-9♥-6♣-2♥ and Mike has A♥-10♥-10♠-3♣. However, Tim's holding includes 8♥-7♥, and Joe has 9-9-8-7. This is one of the worst scenarios for the big draw. Mike's "18 outs" have dropped to only 13. But if all three players go all-in equally, Mike still wins 34.2%, Joe 34.2%, and Tim 31.6%. Remember, they will all likely make a profit due to the money from other players in the pot. Mike's problem is that if he starts raising like there is no tomorrow, and Tim holds only 8-7, he may pass. Now Joe reverts to being a good favorite. With no other information, you need 15 outs against two opponents who both have straights to have the best of it with one card to come.

BLUFFING

When I first played Omaha, I thought bluffing was impossible, because the opposition might well have the hand you were representing. This is not necessarily so, especially shorthanded.

The flop is 10♥-6♥-2♥; you are holding A♥-K♦-Q♣-9♣. In my experience, everybody passes when I have the nut flush and calls when I have the dry ace. It is far more fun to bluff with A♥-K♦-10♠-10♦. If you hold K♥-J♥-10♠-9♥ on this flop and face a bet, it is easier to call, because your third heart makes it more difficult for the bettor to hold the nut flush. Thus the standard joke; if you have a non-nut flush draw, it is better to hold three to the flush. You are first to speak and have flopped a non-nut flush against somebody perfectly capable of bluffing with the lone ace. He bets, you call, and the action is repeated on fourth street. At the death, the board breaks out into an open pair. Now a bet is quite good. He will pass the dry ace (but wouldn't have attempted a third snatch). He may pass the nut flush. If he has a full house, back to the drawing board.

You hold A♥-K♦-Q♣-9♣; the flop is A♠-10♥-2♥. A bet here in late position is a positive play. If a heart comes up, you can represent the nut flush extremely convincingly. You may be winning anyway on the flop. You have three nut-straight drawing cards. With this flop, where there is no action from the others and now the board is A♠-10♥-2♥-7♥, I am deeply suspicious of a bet from the button. If he bets, I will call and call on the river against a reasonable player with a hand such as 2-2. He should have bet A♥-X♥ on the flop. Naturally, I have sometimes checked such hands, hoping the flush will come and that some opponent will read the cards the same way.

Some people feel they must raise all-in on fourth street with the king-high flush. They were going to call on the river anyway. This is a gross blunder. Now the bare ace has nowhere to go except home. He must pass, and you will have burnt up your money against the nuts. Such a play only gains against trips which pass and would have filled up.

You hold J-J-7-4; the flop is K-10-9 offsuit. This isn't a bad bluff shorthanded. You have the blockers. If a caller has trip kings, you can still win legitimately with an 8. A holding of A-J-J-7 would have been nicer, but we can't choose our cards (I hope). If called, you are on your own whether to take the bluff to the river. Since he may be playing the straight passively, my advice is not to do so. It is better to bluff against K-10-9 than K-Q-10. He may get obstinate with a J-9 and you misread his hesitation as a weaker hand. Still worse is betting with just J-J with a flop of 10-9-8; he may hold on with a 7-6.

It is possible to represent from a great depth against a good, but cautious opponent. You hold A♥-K♣-J♦-9♠ with a flop of A♠-Q♥-10♥. He bets; now you raise and are called. He checks and you bet fourth street. The last card is your dream, a heart. Now you bet, and it looks for all the world like you have the flush together with the straight. People are more willing to believe this than a full house if an open pair had come. I don't know why. Note this is a useless ploy if you have run him out of money by fourth street.

Shorthanded I may be prepared to bluff with anything in late position; e.g. A-K-9-8 and a board of Q-Q-10-5. I prefer to make such an outrageous bluff in the steal position, i.e. the hand before the dealer, rather than on the button. This is because everybody knows larceny is in the soul of the player last to speak, and the rotten dogs may even counter-bluff. Even if called, all is not necessarily hopeless; a jack may give me the winning straight. Of course, after the one attempt at the pot, I switch off totally. I am less likely to bluff against Q-10-5-4 offsuit, because my A-K gives me four nut outs, and I don't want to lose that frail chance by being raised. A hand of Q♥-10♣-8♠-2♥ is more likely to elicit a bluff from me. Now I only have three outs, and something seems to send players on a rampage if they call; you make the hand, and then they still call at the river. In addition, a player is now more likely to be on a draw, and can thus be bet out of the pot at the end.

Sometimes miracles happen; e.g. your hand is K-J-J-9 and the flop 8-5-2. You decide to try a steal and get called, but a jack comes up. Alternatively, first a 10 comes, then a queen. Don't be embarrassed. Remember you are absolved of all responsibility when you are bluffing and players come after you. The money has gone; only the poker god can save you. I once held 7-7-6-6 with a board of 9-9-2. The only other player checked. I bet and he called. The next card was (9-9-2) 10. Once again he checked, I bet, and he called. Finally, (9-9-2-10) 8. He checked, and now I had stumbled into a straight. I was able to show it down and win against aces.

Omaha is extremely rich in possibilities. Always be on your guard against unexpected twists, and don't be downhearted. This is not a game for the meek. They are the salt of the earth, but won't inherit the money.

19-POT-LIMIT OMAHA QUIZ
by Stewart Reuben

1. Holding (i) A♠-K♣-J♦-9♥ or (ii) A♠-K♣-J♦-9♠. (a) Facing a raise and reraise before you have ever acted. (b) Having stood a raise or made it yourself and now facing a reraise in the return action. (c) Facing only the blind bet in late position.
(i) and (ii) — (a) Pass (2). Call (0). Raise (-10). It is all too likely you are facing aces and are getting only 3-2 for your money.
(i) — (b) Pass (2). Call (1). Raise (-10). Now you have 2-1 or 3-1 for your money, so a call can be considered.
(ii) — (b) Call (2). Pass (1). Raise (-10). Of course, it depends on the opponent, but not all players reraise just with aces.
(i) and (ii) — (c) Raise (2). Call (0). Pass (-10). Don't be a snivelling, craven coward.

2. Holding 8♣-7♥-6♣-5♥. (a) Facing only the blinds. (b) Facing multihanded action.
(a) Raise (2). Call (1). Pass (-10). You have a premium hand and a raise will disguise it. If you intended to reraise after checking, when somebody else takes action, then we admire your aggressiveness.
(b) Call (2). Raise (0). Pass (-10). A hand as good as this is about as rare as aces double-suited. However, do you really want people to pass? This is a playing hand. All-in you are not a 2-1 dog against aces double-suited. But the back-door draw-outs are relatively minor here. Thus, if there is still action, you have the opportunity to outplay the opposition.

3. Holding (a) A♥-7♣-7♠-2♦ (b) A♥-7♣-7♠-2♥. Facing only the blinds.
(a) Pass (2). Call (0). Raise (-5). In some ways we think a raise is better than a call, if you are trying to snap off the blinds in late position. The hand is junk. It is almost impossible to hit the nuts.

(b) Pass (2). Call (2). Raise (-10). You can hit the nut flush, and once in a blue moon, you will hit such as K♥-7♥-3♠, which is quite exciting. Raising is unwise. A reraise will drive you out.

4. Holding 10-8-7-6 (a) facing only the blinds. (b) facing a bet.
(a) Call (2). Pass (0). Raise (-5). (b) Call (2). Pass (1). Raise (-10). This hand isn't much better than 8-7-6. the broken off spot is too high. 10-9-8-6 is a much better hand.

5. 5♥-4♠-3♥-2♠. (a) Facing only the blinds. (b) Facing a raise with several players still to act.
(a) Call (2). Pass (1). Raise (-9). (b) Pass (2). Call (0). Raise (-10). This is okay for a tiny all-in coup, but with action to come after the flop, it is well-nigh impossible to hit the nuts.

6. J♥-J♣-9♠-6♥ (a) Facing a bet in early position. (b) Facing a bet and raise.
(a) Pass (2). Call (1). Raise (-9) (b) Pass (2). Call (-2). Raise (-10). Basically you are hoping just to hit a Jack. Of course, if you are in a loose game...Change the 6♥ to the 7♥ and your hand is more appetizing. Still, you must pass in (b).

7. This hand made the national press in England, in David Spanier's poker column in "The Independent." We will allow ourselves the privilege of seeing all the cards and deciding what action each player should have taken in this actual hand at the Victoria Casino. Dennis, an extremely solid player, first to speak, holding K-Q-J-9 double-suited.
Raise (2). Call (2). Pass (-10). This is a strong hand, concealed by the early attack. Dennis actually raised.
George, an up-and-down player, holding 7-5-3-2 double-suited.
Raise (-10). Pass (2). Call (-5). George called.
I held 9-9-4-4 single-suited.
Raise (-10). Pass (-2). Call (2). I called.
Donnacha O'Dea, perhaps the best in the British Isles, holding kings single-suited.

Raise (-2). Pass (-10). Call (2). He called.

Derek Webb, solid and astute, holding aces.

Raise (2). Call (0). Pass (-10). He had position with the best hand, and indeed raised.

Back to Dennis, with his K-Q-J-9 double-suited.

Call (2). Pass (-2). Raise (-10). Derek doesn't have to have aces, and this hand is still extremely strong. He called.

Now George, with his 7-5-3-2 double-suited.

Call (-10). Pass (2). Raise (-20). This hand has far too many gaps. George should have passed, but was no doubt seduced by the thought that most players had high cards.

I, with two pair; 9-9-4-4 single-suited.

Call (2). Pass (2). Raise (-20). Basically I must hope to flop a set, about 22%. I was getting 4-1 for my money. This is rather marginal, and a pass would have been more discreet than my actual call.

Donnacha, with his pair of kings. If he called, the pot would be $1000, and he had only $500 left. Everybody else was playing with much more money.

Call (2). Raise (0). Pass (10). Donnacha actually raised. We hesitate to criticize, but if Derek just calls, the other three will follow suit. If Derek raises, he has aces, and the best Donnacha can hope for is to be left alone, a severe underdog. Why not take the flop?

The pot now stood at $1500. Derek had $2500 left.

Raise (2). Call (-3). Pass (-20). Of course Derek raised all-in, the full pot, with his aces.

Dennis had $14,000 left.

Call (2). Pass (2). Raise (-10). The hand is becoming rather marginal.

George had $2800 left.

Call (-10) Pass (2). Raise (-12). The odds just aren't there. I had more than $14,000 left.

Raise (2). Pass (2). Call (-2). The two pair is dubbed "Donnacha's hand" in England. This is because he once explained, "I don't want to play guessing games with this holding. I want to see all five cards." Basically two pair make trips about 34% of the time by the end of the pot. Of course they may not win. The pot stood at $9000 and it was $2500 to me. Clearly I have pot odds—if I can reach the river. Donnacha is almost certainly marked with kings, else why did he not raise first time round? Derek has aces. George's hand is a mystery. But Dennis's is clearly a drawing hand. Any such holding must be less than even money against any pair. I had to be blocking Dennis's with at least two cards. It is a **much** better play for me to raise than just call. In fact, passing is better than calling. So I raised the pot of $11,500.

Dennis, hanging on.

Pass (2). Call (-2). Dennis should have realized at least six of the cards he was seeking were held by other players. Derek is marked with aces, Donnacha with kings, and I am marked with another picture pair and probably two other such cards. But the heat of the battle went to Dennis's head and he called. Naturally, George called for his last $300.

The boardcards: A 6 6 8 2. Thus Derek and I each made a profit of about $8,800. Had Dennis played correctly and passed, I would have lost $2500. Dennis grumpily observed that he would have won the side pot if a K, Q or J had come at any stage, and predicted that I would go broke in less than a year. We draw no conclusions. But Donnacha would have played more accurately with more money, and I needed to cover the table for my arguably foolhardy play.

8. Holding A♠–K♥–K♣–2♠. Flop K♠–9♠–4♠. Nobody has acted.

Bet (2). Check (2). Nobody is going to bet for you here, or on fourth street. Checking will result in your winning a small pot ultimately. A bet may elicit a call from a flush or trips and lead to a big win—but probably not.

9. A♥–10♠–8♥–5♠ with a flop of Q♣-J♠-9♣. (a) everybody so far has checked. (b) there has been a bet and a call.

(a) Bet (2). Check (0). Now, if somebody raises, you can pass content in the knowledge you are losing. If you wait for somebody else to bet, they may be on a steal, or have the same hand as you.

(b) Pass (2). Call (0). Raise (-5). You may still be winning and you can hit the nut top straight, but let discretion be the better part of valor.

10. J-J-8-4 with a flop of A-K-J. Facing a bet.
Pass (2). Call (-1). Raise (-5). It doesn't matter how many people are in the pot or anything. The fact is, you have fourth best. It is quite likely the bettor has opened up with higher trips.

11. A♠-A♥-Q♦-4♦ with a flop of 10♦-9♦-4♥. Facing several checks and no action.
Check (2). Bet (-1). This is an action-packed flop. Somebody is probably lurking in the weeds, and may not even raise with trip 10's. You have only one nut out, the A♣. If you face a bet, pass.

12. J-10-8-7 with a flop of 9-6-2. (a) If checked to. (b) Having been bet at, with several other players to come.
(a) Bet (2). Check (1). You have 13 outs and can stand a raise.
(b) Call (2). Raise (0). Pass (-5). Any of the straightening cards leaves you with overcards. Thus, another drawing player may be welcome. If you raise and get reraised, that's a great deal of money to have splashing around with a hand that is an underdog to trips.

13. Q-10-9-8 with a flop of K♥-7♥-6♠. Facing a bet and raise.
Pass (2). Call (0). Raise (-5). You have 13 outs, but only 9 are the nuts, due to the flush-draw. A reraise will not put that hand out. Therefore, the most probable scenario is that you are going to have to run over both trips and a flush draw. Why put yourself in such an unenviable situation?

14. Holding J-10-9-7 suited. You have called a raise and then been reraised before the flop, which is 10-6-4. It is checked to you and only the last raiser remains. There is only enough money left on the table for one final bet.
Bet (2). Check (1). Against dry aces you have 15 outs. What is more, you may secure the pot uncontested. To check and call a bet

is disgustingly bad poker. If this was your intention, deduct ten points. Frankly, you are supposed to play in this type of situation even without the middle-straight possibility.

15. Q♥-10♥-9♣-8♦. Board (7♥-6♣-2♦) 5♥. You stood a bet and raise with this hand on the flop. Now the 5♥ has arrived, and the first player has bet, while the second has called.
Raise (2). Call (-2). Pass (-10). A player with trips must be pushed out. You have only four nut improving cards, but a backdoor Queen-high flush is very substantial.

16. In the above example, what if the first player reraises and the second passes?
Call (2). Raise (0). Pass (-10). It is possible you still have more draw-out cards than your opponent. Alternatively, he may have the straight plus trips, or the dreaded A♥-10♣-9♥-8♠. It is impossible to construct a hand where he has 13 advantage cards on you. Also a reraise, likely to be all-in, would sacrifice the advantage you have of position.

17. K♥-Q♠-10♥-10♠. Board 10♣-8♥-2♠-9♥. You did your duty before the flop and raised with good position. You carried on with the good work and bet out on the flop. Now there is a bet and raise before it ever comes to you, the last player in the hand.
Call (2). Raise (2). Pass (-5). You are going to have to stand all the heat. You should win with two jacks (the other two should be in their hands), any pair (although they probably have one 9 each) and all the hearts. This comes to 18 cards! If you raise, they will probably calm down and just call. You want all the money in.

18. K♠-K♥-8♠-7♥. Board (10♣-9♦-2♣) 6♦. There has been action in the pot after the flop and now you lead out. The sole remaining player raises you.
Pass (2). Call (1). Raise (-100). You idiot! A pass was correct on the flop. You only had three nut outs; both a king and a jack might

have made higher straights. Now see what a fine mess you've got yourself into. He's even got position.

19. A♦-Q♥-J♠-7♦. Board 10♦ 7♣ 4♦ A♥ 7♠. Throughout the pot, you have only been up against an astute player who respects you. You checked the flop and he bet. Fourth street you bet out and he calls. On the river you check and he bets out.
Raise (2). Call (-2). Pass (1). He could have fours full, but the most likely explanation is he has tens full. From his viewpoint you could have made aces full or four 7's. He is probably going to pass.

20. K-10-9-8. Flop J-7-6. No action to you, late in hand.
Bet (2). Check (0). You have 13 nut outs.

21. Same hand. Board (J-7-6) Q. You bet last time, had one caller who now checks.
Bet (2). Check (-1). You have 20 outs, of which only 6 are not the nuts.

22. Same hand. Board (J-7-6) Q 2, you having bet fourth street. He checks.
Bet (2). Check (-2). He may have a drawing hand and you are winning. Alternatively, he may have a three-card drawing hand and a pair. He may wilt under the pressure with J-7. Sadly, he may call and you can talk about another Big Beat—if that turns you on.

23. K♥-Q♠-10♦-9♥. Board J♥ 7♥ 3♥ 4♦ 9♠. You bet in late position and were raised by the button. You called. You also called on fourth street. On the river, the pot is $2,000 and there is only $300 left to bet.
Check (2). Bet (-100). We have seen the mistake of betting many, many times by seemingly sensible people. They reason, "I will have to call, so I may as well bet it." But he will only call with the nut flush. You know he almost surely has the A♥, but he may be bluffing with the dry ace. You must leave him room to bluff. If you choose to put the $300 in, this should be done on fourth street,

when if he can fill up, you are making him pay. Had an open pair appeared on the river, you could have tried betting the $300, representing a full house. You may be bluffing at nothing and he might pass the nut flush. Of course, bluffing is much more likely to succeed if you have a fair-sized cannon to fire.

Score	Comments
85-96	Find yourself the biggest game you can afford.
65-84	You still have some technical problems. Be careful!
40-64	Play very small Omaha and then reread this book.
0-39	You haven't grasped the nuances of the game.
Less than 0	Play only for match-sticks or chocolate money.

20-SEVEN-CARD STUD
"The overlay is of paramount importance"

by Stewart Reuben

A great deal has been written about this game when played with a limit betting structure. I have assumed you are familiar with that form of the game.

The high card usually starts the ball rolling in seven stud pot-limit. This is to help prevent the pot getting too large too soon. Most people play conservatively on third street, and there is seldom a double-raise at this stage. Thus, the pot grows only gradually in size. Even in small games there may be betting at the river.

Over 20 years ago I played the following hand against Jack. Card four I held (7 7) K 7 against (? ?) 8♣ 4♣. The pot was $3 and I bet $2, which he called. Pot size now $7.

Card five I had (7 7) K 7 9 and Jack (? ?) 8♣ 4♣ K♣. I was first to speak and might have made a gesture of impatience. He may have bet out of turn, overlooking the fact that my 9 made me high. He bet $4. The rules were very strict in England at that time; if he bet out of turn, he was barred from betting or raising on that card. The dealer asked whether I had checked. I genuinely answered I didn't know. "What do you mean, you don't know?" queried the dealer. "What I said, but I condone the bet and call." The dealer was mollified, play continued, and now the pot stood at $15.

Card six (7 7) K 7 9 7 and Jack (? ?) 8♣ 4♣ K♣ 2♦. I checked and he bet $15, which I called. The pot was now $45.

On the river I squeezed my last card, but as I hadn't improved, I checked. He bet $45 and I raised $135, which he called. Thus, there was a total of $405 in the pot. Note the effect of that $4 bet. Without it, the pot would have been only $189. Jack lost $108 more than if there had been no bet card five.

When I told a soft, tight player this anecdote he said, "A check would have suited you down to the ground on fifth street." Forget about how things actually turned out. I suspect he is mathematically wrong. My potential win from the $4 investment was far greater than the actual small sum under consideration.

We have seen at least eight-fold inflation in Britain since then, but the game is still played by much the same players with the same stakes as before. Thus, unfortunately, the game is played too small now to attract me. In earlier days I used to win extremely regularly, such that for some years my hourly rate was $9. Even after a losing session, I could go home and think, "I played five hours, therefore I've won $45." Invariably at the year's end this was proven to be more-or-less correct.

Most players cannot bring themselves to play in a smaller game. This is the "macho" principle. Somehow it reflects on their manliness to drop a notch. It is noticeable some of the best Vegas players don't have this hang-up, especially when they have been running bad. I used not to mind at all playing small while waiting for the big game. It kept me away from the blackjack table, where I at best break even. Now I am more reluctant to expend energy on a game where I figure only to win small.

The great thing about seven-card stud is that it is a perfect game for winning. If you can gauge the playing strength of your opponent and provided he isn't an extremely good player, you can come out ahead over a period of time almost regardless of what cards you've been dealt. I am sufficiently arrogant to believe I can virtually give a card start to certain tight, soft players. (I would never claim this against a wild, loose player.)

The wild ones are much more dangerous and will often win money from me—even though, in the long run, they may be bigger losers than players of the first profile. Generally speaking, it is essential to play much closer to standard trick-free poker against very weak or very strong opposition. The weak players may have your intricate maneuvers simply go over their head, whereas the strong may pick up on what you are doing.

HOW TO PLAY CARD THREE

1. As in limit poker, play only with trips, a pair, three to a flush or three to an up-and-down straight. Last in hand against only the forced bet, a call with a live ace in the hole or such as 10 9 7 with all J 8 6 live can be considered. Naturally, you may raise on any holding you like. A bet or raise can be made with any cards in poker; a call must be with a genuine hand.

2. Raising with three to a flush or straight constitutes a bluff. The action is mathematically unsound. Three to a flush is roughly 3-1 against making a four-flush if your hand is fully live, although the pairing possibilities makes it nearly even money to improve. If you are reraised and call, the pot is probably getting too big for the amount of money left to win. Also, if you do make a four-flush, usually you want several players in the pot.

3. A concealed pair is significantly more valuable than if split. Thus (3 3) 7 is better than (7 3) 3. This partly because of the explosive nature of mystery trips and partly because it is easier to hit a 7 than a 3. If you do so, you may well secure the pot on fourth street. With two small pair, this is often the best result.

4. Secondary holdings with the pair are much less important than in limit. The starting hands 6 6 A or 8♣ 8♠ 9♣ have a special resonance. But in pot-limit, you may be all-in before they become relevant.

5. If you are playing in a game where the low card brings it in, then if you are the only person left, everybody else having folded, all you need to raise is a dry king, three-flush or three-straight. This will include your percentage of bluffs.

6. In limit poker it is received wisdom that buried aces or kings are better slowplayed. This is because you tend to win small pots or lose large ones with such holdings. If the pot is large, they are impossible to release with only a limit bet. In pot-limit you can protect your hand. Also, you can muck them if

things go wrong. Thus, fast action with big pairs is much more sensible.

7. Again, the advice in limit is to play the hell out of your low trips. Now the rewards are far greater for slowplaying such a hand.

Because I take ferocious action even with quite mediocre holdings, I can fast-play my monsters as well. One of the joys of poker is that players have different styles. What can be right for one player may be totally wrong for another.

HOW TO PLAY CARD FOUR

1. Muck junk as rapidly as possible.

2. The potential overlay of a hand like 10♠ 9♠ is gigantic. Any card A through 6 plus the 5♠, 4♠, 3♠, 2♠ can be hit to strike fear into your opponent. Beware of an aggressive player who checks such a hand. He probably intends to check-raise or slowplay a monster.

3. A four-flush is at least as good a hand as a pair of aces. It is true the flush draw only makes it 48% of the time, but sometimes the player makes a winning two pair anyway.

Basically I want to avoid an all-in coup where I hold such as (A 4) A 9 against a four-flush. This is giving the opposition even money. Thus I am **more** likely to bet fourth street than check-raise. If my opponent bets and I raise, then the pot is often big enough for him to reraise all-in. If I have bet and he raises, then I can call. Next card I can set him in if he hits a blank and have the best of it, or pass if he improves. If he hits an open pair, I may pass my dry aces. His weakest hand is probably a four-flush and a pair, and that is favorite against my hand. Naturally, two pair or trips are favorite against a four-flush, but it isn't that big a deal.

4. When you first play all poker variations, it is best to learn how to play tight. Later on you can learn to play loose, but the option to fall back is always there.

If your opponent has an open pair against your four-flush, then potentially he has a full house, and you are drawing to lose. Similarly, if a player is already in the pot with what looks like a four-flush, then four to an up-and-down straight is a losing tight situation. You may both improve with an extremely traumatic result. However, one of the main benefits of a straight is that people are much less ready to believe in them than flushes. Thus, you are more likely to be paid off when it does blossom.

5. Against a good player it is sometimes worth calling with a hand such as (Q J) 10 8 or (Q J) 10 9 facing an open pair of 8's. This is again because you are more likely to get paid off. The anomalous nature of your hand will pass over the head of a weakie. The above middle-pin straight is a better proposition than (Q 8) 10 J because now a 9 isn't so obvious a middle-pin.

6. One important principle of pot limit is that although aces may be a slight favorite against one flush-draw, they are a big dog against two flush-draws. Thus, suppose you bet with (A 6) A 4, one player raises with (? ?) 9♣ 7♣, and the next reraises with (? ?) Q♦ 5♦. It is correct to pass. Overall, they both miss only 25% of the time. When looking down the barrels of the guns of two players each with an open two-flush, it may be wise to check a high pair. But I prefer to bet, and then run for the hills when the going gets rough.

This principle of the made hand being an underdog to two players each on a draw can apply even on fifth street. Player A has (J 10) 9 8 7. Player B (A♥ A♠) 6♠ 2♠ A♣. Player C (Q Q) Q 5 4. In an all-in coup, Player B has the best of it. He wins 41.3%, Player A 33.5%, and Player C 25.2%. The three flush helps Player B. The whole situation is quite different from a game such as Omaha. Here the likelihood of one player improving hardly impinges on the other player's chances.

Note that if the pot stands at $100, Player A bets $90 all-in, and Player B calls all-in, then Player C is correct to call, even if the players turn their cards over and show him he is beaten in two spots. He wins 25.2% of the time, and will win $280 for his $90 wager.

7. A hand worth mentioning in poker mythology is an open-end straight-flush draw such as (7♣ 6♣) 9♣ 8♣. This is so likely to improve, with 15 outs on each of three cards, that it scores 48.5% against trips on fourth street. But don't hold your breath; it is 2500-1 against being dealt this hand. Last time it happened to me I was up against aces with only one club and no 4s or 10s showing or passed in a ninehanded game. All the money went in. At the end of the hand, I was the proud possessor of (7♣ 6♣) 9♣ 8♣ 4♠ 3♦ 2♠, a 9-high. That's what I call going down in style!

HOW TO PLAY CARDS FIVE AND SIX

1. The initiative is so vital in pot-limit poker that the overlay is totally dominant. Even if it seems ridiculous, e.g. 6 2 3 offsuit, it is still possible for these cards to form a straight. If your board does not hold a superior possibility, you must proceed with extreme caution. Many people become confused. A♣ 7♣ 2♣ does not overlay 9 4 4. The latter could be a full house. Whoever is in the driving seat can check-raise, bet out, or check-pass his hand at will.

Thus, if you hold (? ?) 7♣ 10♣ Q♦ against (? ?) 9 8 7 and hit a club, players are ready to believe you have a flush, and will put down their hands like little children. If you hit an open pair, they are much less ready to believe a full house. Why this is so must remain an eternal mystery.

2. Against a fairly good player, you can bet not only the overlay but also the underlay. I was having dinner with my friend Frank Thompson, and I explained to him I did this about once a month against our mutual acquaintance, Len. e.g. Len (? ?) A bets. I call with (7 2) 7. There may or may not be other people in the pot. Card 4 Len with (? ?) A 9 bets; I with (7 2) 7♣ 3♥ call. Card 5 Len (? ?) A 9 3 bets and we are the only two players left in the pot. Now I with (7 2) 7♣ 3♥ Q♠ raise. Note, we must each have a large sum of money left so that there is still a great

deal of betting possible, and particularly that I do not have a two-flush or even two-straight showing. Otherwise, I may be on a draw-and-pair.

What is Len to make of this? Obviously I have a strong hand which I am willing to take up against aces. Thus he would normally pass. Remember my pair of 7's may have been winning. Len was much too good a player to be always betting with a good hand only. One day all three of us were playing and this sequence occurred. Frank said after Len passed, "I didn't believe you when you told me about that coup." Len, no fool, said, "Well, he doesn't get rich off me" (which was perfectly true). Frank later apologized and said he owed me a dinner.

3. Do not bet or raise if you are frightened of a reraise. e.g. You hold (7♣ 5♣) K♣ 7♦ Q♣ 4♠ against (? ?) A 9 6 4. He checked on fourth and fifth streets and you bet each time. If he checks on sixth street, check straight back. If you bet and he raises, you must pass. You are only going to win with a flush or possibly trips. Thus your bet, rather than taking off a free card, has escalated the pot, and now it is too large to stomach coming in for the out-draw.

Consider on the other hand (A 9) 9 3 A 4 against (? ?) 7♣ A♣ K♣ 6♥ where he has just called your bets on third, fourth, and fifth streets. Now he checks, you bet, and he reraises all-in. You can pass with fair confidence that you are losing; no regrets. All you have passed up with your apparently rash bet is an approximately 10% chance of an out-draw. Had you checked, you might have let him out-draw you for free, where he would have passed—now there's a real nightmare!

4. Yes, in the above sequence, he may have bluffed you out. Few people will check-raise as a bluff. This is partly because they do not have the heart for it, and partly because it is mathematically unsound. The pot is $100. He checks and you bet $100. Now he calls and raises $300. He is risking $400 to win $200.

5. Naturally the greatest difficulty lies with marginal hands. It's easy to play the nuts, but that isn't usually what gets the money. In poker generally, **if you can't lose, you can't win much.**

The great difference between pot-limit and limit seven card stud is that when in doubt at pot-limit, you should pass. The downside risk is gigantic. If you call reluctantly on fifth street, then you may face three times the bet on sixth street, and nine times on the river. It is essential to be able to release a hand. It is equally essential not to be pushed around. It is your poker judgment that is going to make you a winner or loser. Poker is not a game of absolutes. If when high, you check a marginal hand and show weakness, then it is extremely difficult to make the correct decision when bet at. Thus, I prefer to bet, and pass a raise. Soft check-call doesn't hack it in any game.

6. Sometimes you will encounter a player so loose and aggressive that the best way to play him is simply to check and call. Occasionally he will have you beaten and you will go off in a big way, but that's poker. If possible, sit to the immediate right of such a player. Then all his bets go through the rest of the table, and you can safely prepare a check-raise of the other players, or pass if discretion proves to be the better part of valor.

There was one Englishman against whom I adopted the system that, if I had a pair, I would still call at the river unless his board beat me. One day I mustered a pair of fives. The action wasn't that fierce, and the pot was fairly small when he bet on seventh street. My fives hadn't improved, and after all, they probably aren't favorite against seven random cards. I thought, "If I don't pass this, he may realize he can never bluff me." So I reluctantly passed. He heaved a sigh of relief, saying, "I thought I could never get you out." This is the only example I know of a trap pass at poker.

7. Multihanded action pots are quite different in pot-limit from limit poker. You hold (A 4) A 9 6 against Sid who shows (? ?) 4 7 7 and Jim (? ?) Q K 2. Sid leads off. At limit poker, you

should raise in order to eliminate Jim and get heads-up against a probable two pair, or possibly pair plus up-and-down straight. In pot-limit you should either pass or call. A raise is appallingly dangerous.

8. The whole problem of whether you have adequate odds to call an all-in bet against a hand you "know" to be beating you is considered in the chapters on odds.

If there are two people in the pot and one has bet, while the next has limped in, then it is okay to call with a four-flush, especially if it is something like (K♣ 7♣) 4♣ A♦ 9♣ 3♥, where you bluffed on fourth street. You are about 4-1 against making the flush, and you have only 3-1 for your money, but you have good implied odds. i.e. If you hit the flush, there is a very fair chance you will be paid off.

9. Whether you should call a pot bet from one opponent at sixth street to make an outdraw is less clear. Let me first recount the most extraordinary pot I've been involved in. It may have no educational value, but it is my favorite story. Normally I charge $25 to listen to a big beat.

Card three I was forced to bring it in with (6♠ 4♠) A♥. Several people called, but the A♣ passed. Card four I held (6♠ 4♠) A♥ A♦ and Hungarian Lou held (? ?) J♣ 7♣. I bet most of the pot and Lou and one other player called. Card five I had (6♠ 4♠) A♥ A♦ A♠. Lou showed (? ?) J♣ 7♣ 3♣. The third party was irrelevant. I bet part of the pot and Lou raised the maximum. This is an unusual play with a flush against open trips, but perfectly sound. I was forced in at card three and thus can be played for random holecards. The A♣ has passed, and thus it is nearly 15-1 against a hidden pair. I called. This is correct. I have a fair chance of improving and should get the lot if I do. The pot stood at $300.

Card six I held (6♠ 4♠) A♣ A♦ A♠ K♠ against (? ?) J♣ 7♣ 3♣ Q♣. Lou bet $300 after my check. Now I may not only hit a full house but also a winning flush, a total of 18 outs. I am sufficiently close to even money to raise all-in. This wouldn't be a bad bluff, except I knew Lou would call with his flush. Also he will call on the last card if I improve.

Card seven: I didn't improve and checked. Our Hungarian friend set himself in for $900 and I passed. Lou now displayed his three holecards. Not a club among them, nor could he even beat a pair of aces! What a magnificently impossible coup! Now the pundits climbed over themselves to declare that I shouldn't have called card six and then passed; or that I should have called on seventh street, as it was an obvious bluff. Nobody would bet a flush. What hopeless gibberish.

Let us consider the more mundane (K K) 4 7 K 9 against (? ?) 5♣ 8♣ Q♣ 2♣. The pot is $1000, which he bets. Should you call? It is about 3-1 against improving. Thus, if you figure he has a flush, and he is all-in, the hand must be passed. If he still has money, then it is a winning proposition to call and bet out if you fill. The made flush almost never passes. If he was bluffing, it may seem as if there is no problem. However, if you fail to fill and check, he will bet, and you should almost invariably pass. Strangely enough, if you make your full house and check, a strong player may well check back his flush in case you are sandbagging. Thus, paradoxically, you actually may prefer your opponent to be beating you rather than bluffing. It would be ideal if the player with the possible flush had about $3000 left. Then, when you trap-check with the house, it is correct for him to go all-in, as he has no need to fear a reraise.

Clearly, life would be easier if he were first to speak; perhaps in our example having hit the A♣ instead of the 2♣. Then at the river, if he bets, you have your odds by calling with a full house; never mind about raising. If he checks, you bet the pot and there you are.

Another problem now arises if you both have unlimited funds. I once held (4♣ 3♣) 5♣ 8♣ A♣ Q♠ against Sid, a tight, solid player with (? ?) 4 7 9 K. To my surprise I was called at card six, so that the pot held $3000. I have long since given up trying to outplay this opponent, and bet $1500 blind, allowing him to know this. He hesitated, dwelt for a long time, and finally called. I realized what had happened. He had improved and decided not to raise. He reckoned I might hold three aces and would have no call. The only result from his raise would be a reraise if I improved. What is more, he knew I was perfectly capable of, and therefore was frightened of, my raising **without** the full house, as a bluff. I announced my flush, and to my horror, turned over the straight flush, having hit the 2♣. Had I bet the pot or checked, I would have been sure to win $3000. It was not a mistake for him to call sixth street, even though his hand didn't merit a raise once made. It was eminently possible I was on a bluff, betting my overlay. He might well have called at the river, even if he failed to improve. By the way, Sid's actual holding was 4 4 4 7 7.

I once had the following against a Canadian who may have been the tightest, dullest, softest player I have ever met. (10♣ 10♠) 10♦ J♦ 10♥ Q♦. He held (? ?) 4 A 7 9. To my surprise, he called the $1000 bet on sixth street. Clearly three aces was the only possible hand. What's more, he would pass on the river, irrespective of the size of my bet, unless he improved. After the last card I bet $3000, he raised $9000, and I set him in for $2000 more, which he called.

Now I blundered and pontificated, "You need the fourth ace to win." He left the game and never returned. What a loss! Usually you can't win much from such players, and they may simply be wasting a seat, but they are a steady and certain source of income. Two players, Frank Thompson and Sid, told me later that once I had bet $3000, they wouldn't have raised. Clearly, I was either bluffing, in which case a raise is pointless, or I could beat aces full. As I've already said, there are certain players I cannot outplay. Anybody who claims he would pass aces full for $2000 in a $29,000 pot is full of hot air.

When you have a monster, betting out wins more than a trap-check against another enormous hand. The most common decision you will have to make is how to play either side of the following: Jim (K 7) K 9 8 4 against Tim (A 9) A♣ 7♣ Q♥ 5♦. Tim should usually bet. He cannot risk checking, giving Jim a free card and then facing a genuine bet at the river—which for all he knows is a bluff. Jim has the problem that Tim may be betting on the come with a four-flush. There are no panaceas here. You must simply take a view. If there are players in the pot after you, and you are in doubt, a pass is the best policy.

11. One common error is that people feel they are absolutely committed, so if they call on sixth street, then they must call on the river. Personally, when I am calling against what I hope is a bluff, and if it isn't, then I can still outdraw, I tend to let my mind go blank at this point. I genuinely don't know my final intended action. Sometimes the vibes seem to come through as to what is the correct move. Perhaps the opponent's body language gives a clue.

Incidentally, when I have taken action with a strong hand, should I be thinking to myself, "Call, call, call" and with a bluff, "Pass, pass, pass", or is it the other way round? The jury is still out on this one.

HOW TO PLAY THE RIVER

1. If you have a fairly good hand and you believe you are up against a drawing hand, it is usually best to check—blind or not, as you wish. This is because, if you bet, you aren't giving him enough room to bluff. Time and again I have heard the asinine comment when somebody bet all-in and was called by the drawing hand which has hit, "I bet because I would have had to call anyway."

2. If you have a fairly good hand and fear a pot-size bet, it is sometimes advisable to make a partial bet; e.g. there is $1000 in the middle, then bet $400. If you are now raised by a moderate player, he has certainly improved. In order for this play to be effective, you must occasionally make such a bet with a really good hand. Otherwise, people will catch on to it.

3. If you have called on sixth street and are now afraid to bet on the end after improving, you have made a serious blunder. Many is the time I have called on sixth street, and when my opponent has come out betting at the river, almost wanted to pass blind, rather than look and find I'd improved enough to see more money go down the drain.

4. One principal reason for betting before seventh street is the fear of being outdrawn. I had aces up against Jim. On sixth street it was clear he had made a flush. I had no open pair and checked. There was $500 in the pot. To my surprise he checked back. I checked on the last card, he bet the pot, and I raised the maximum $1500. He called and I showed a full house. This was purely gratuitous. I had no intention of calling for a 9-1 shot on the previous card, nor of calling with just aces up at the river.

His idea of checking on sixth street and giving me a free card is a clever one. Against a player who doesn't realize he has a flush, he has an excellent chance of being paid off. The opponent has only to risk $500 instead of potentially $2000. The problem arose when I check-raised at the end. I am capable of trying to bluff out a flush when facing the right opponent. I am entitled to get paid. This demonstrates it is no good being too fancy with tough, aggressive players. In big-bet poker just snatch off whatever you can from them and concentrate on the mug punters.

An error at big-bet poker is much more costly than at limit poker. Thus the game tends to be played more slowly and carefully, though not necessarily with less action. It is much easier to get out of it in pot-limit, just as it is easier to become comprehensively stuck in a quagmire which may or may not be of your own making.

5. Naturally, the pot quite often doesn't get as far as card seven before everybody is all-in. The Combustion Point arises early on. Thus, you have jacks up and think you are facing aces with two cards to come. What are you waiting for? He bets; raise all-in and be done with it. If you are correct, you don't much

mind whether he calls or passes. Just don't be a wimp and a calling station and call, call, call until you have been outdrawn.

The fact is, you can play perfectly and lose even **without** the dreaded out-draw. Some people think the out-draw diminishes the game. They aren't thinking correctly. Without the chance of improving, there would be no poker action.

6. Seven-card stud has the exciting facet that the players may turn up with amazing holecards. Whenever I hit a monster, I consider very carefully whether there is any way I can be beaten. This slight hesitation sometimes leads to people calling.

The following is a true story. Michael (? ? ?) 3 3 3 K against Joan (? ? ?) 5 9 5 4. Presumably there had been some betting prior to the river card. On seventh street there was ferocious action and all the money went in. "Give me the money," shouted the exultant Joan with four 5's. "No, give me the money," exclaimed Michael, showing down four kings.

I wasn't there, but the question posed was, "How many raises would you put in against Stewart with four 5's?" Clearly I am renowned as a swashbuckler. Joan must have trip threes beaten on sixth street. Michael will not bet less than 3's full. Personally I wouldn't bet even with that; it is too marginal. Thus Joan must have at least 5's full to raise. Again, I would probably be more circumspect. For Michael to reraise, he must have a minimum of kings full. Joan's second raise indicates four 5's. Now Michael's next raise **must** be four kings. If Joan were really a good player, she should pass that last raise. Mind you, I don't think I would have been good enough.

21-SEVEN-CARD STUD QUIZ
by Stewart Reuben

1. Holding (Q♣ 2♣) 7♣, facing a raise with two clubs showing.

Pass (2). Call (0). Raise (-10)
The probability of your making a flush is poor.

2. (6♣ 6♠) 3♥, facing a bet.

Call (2). Raise (0). Pass (0)
This is an ideal pair. If you hit it, the hand appears to be on a draw.

3. (A A) K, against an ace. You have raised and he reraised.

Reraise (2). Call (1). Pass (-100)
You cannot be losing, or even be an underdog. If he holds such as A A J, you are a substantial favorite, but still wouldn't mind a pass. If he doesn't have aces, you don't know where he's at, and this is more dangerous. Pity if he folds.

4. (8 7) 9, with no cards 5 through Jack showing, facing a raise.

Call (2). Raise (-10). Pass (1)
You certainly do not want to generate action with this hand; it breaks off too readily.

5. (A♣ 4♣) 7♣ 10♣. (a) facing a check. (b) facing a bet.

(a) Bet (2). Check (0)
You may win the pot there and then. If not, what the hell, you are very strong. A check really counts as a slowplay.
(b) Call (2). Raise (2). Pass (-10)
If there are players to come, it is good to call and encourage them to join the party. It is also good to go to war. This assumes no open pair and plenty of clubs left.

6. (8 6) 7 9, facing a bet from the high card and a raise from (? ?) 2♣ Q♣.

Pass (2). Call (1). Raise (-10)
You are fighting fire when armed with only a puny extinguisher. A four-straight is a big underdog to a four-flush. It isn't so great against two pair either. However, if you hit it next card, you are going to get action; people do not fear straights.

7. (A♥ 7♥) Q♥ 10♥, Facing a bet from (? ?) 7 7.

Call (2). Pass (2). Raise (1)
Against certain tight players it is correct to pass, but you do have one of your opponent's cards. Raising is misleading and calling is natural.

8. (7 7) A 4, facing a bet from (? ?) 7 7.

Raise (2). Call (-2). Pass (2)
If you call, and your opponent bets again, then your only hope is to raise. Then the pot is huge. It is better in this situation to blast away and hope to win immediately. Passing may well be best of all.

9. (K 7) 7 9 K 2, facing a bet from (? ?) A 6 5 10 who has been betting all the way.

Raise (2). Call (0). Pass (-1)
Your hand looks extremely innocuous and could be a four-straight. He may well still be betting with bare aces. If he reraises, I am happy to pass—although I have lost my small shot at a full house.

10. (K 7) K♦ 9♦ Q Q, against (? ?) A 4 2 9. You called his bet on fourth and fifth street. Now you bet and he raises.

Raise (2). Call (2). Pass (2)
It all depends on the opposition. He may be putting you on a four-flush and be raising with dry aces. He may have you beaten. You may be able to blast him out with your overlay. Chess is a great game; if you want an exact science, stick to that.

11. (A 7 2) A 9 Q 7, against (? ? ?) 9♠ 2♦ 10♠ 4♣.

Bet the pot (0). Bet small (1). Check (2)
Nothing shows the difference from limit poker better. In that game, nobody would try to rip off the ace, so that there is no serious chance of a bluffing bet on the river. Thus you bet for a call from two pair in that game. Here, if you bet out, you are unlikely to get action except from a hand beating you. A small bet often shows more weakness than a check. If you check, you may snap off a bluff or a bet from two pair.

12. (9♣ 2♣ Q♣) 4♣ 5♣ 9♥ Q♠, against (? ? ?) 9 10 8 7. Earlier in the pot you were quite active. Now you check at the river; he bets, you raise and he reraises.

Call (1). Pass (2). Raise (-20)
Your opponent looks for all the world like a straight, but he could hold 8 7 in the hole and have hit a full house. Since he knows he has a transparent looking straight, and yet you are raising, it is most unwise for you to reraise him. This is an apple-juice hand. Against the correct opponent, it is best to pass.

13. (4 4 9) 6 2 6 6, against (? ? ? ?) Q♥ 6♥ 7 Q. You have bet fifth and sixth streets.

Check (2). Bet (0)
It is obvious you are full. Be prepared to pass if he bets.

Score	**Comment**
25-28	Congratulations, you have graduated.
18-24	We can all learn, but you are ready to play.
12-17	Play in small games for the moment.
0-11	Is this really your metier?
Less than 0	Buy another copy of this book. It is a better way to spend your money.

22-LOWBALL DRAW
"Bluff Instead of Showing Down a Sure Loser"

by Bob Ciaffone

Pot-limit lowball draw (and its close cousin no-limit lowball draw) is an excellent gambling game. Most forms of poker tend to have their bluffing done early in a hand, where the bluffer has some kind of drawing hand that can still get lucky and win. In contrast, the bulk of the bluffing at lowball draw is done after you bust out. The typical situation is a one-card draw that pairs, especially a hand making a nearly hopeless higher pair such as sevens. A person with very little bluff in him can sometime survive at a game such as Omaha, but he is dead meat in a lowball game.

There are two kinds of draw poker that are commonly played. The game of Ace-to-Five lowball does not have straights and flushes count against you, so the best hand is 5-4-3-2-A, a "wheel." It is more often than not played with a joker, called "the bug," which counts as the lowest card not making a pair. The other form of lowball is Deuce-to-Seven, where an ace is only a high card, and straights or flushes ruin a hand's value. The best hand here is 7-5-4-3-2.

This chapter's approach is to discuss hands as if the game were Ace-to-Five. At the very end of the chapter, I'll tell you what adjustments to make for Deuce-to-Seven play. I also think it better to assume the game is no-limit, which is probably the more frequent betting structure.

In California, and occasionally elsewhere, the game of limit lowball is quite often played with a rule that you must bet a seven or better hand after the draw. To check there guarantees an eight or worse. The merit of this rule may be debated at limit play, but for no-limit, it is clearly very bad. To give someone the knowledge that they have a lock hand when the enemy checks is definitely not in the spirit of no-limit gambling.

Let us assume we are playing in a seven-handed no-limit Ace-to-Five game where the bug is in use. The game is usually played pass-and-out; before the draw you must either open or fold. What do you need to open?

In early position, the values are pretty much the same as in limit poker. You need at least a one-card draw at a seven, or a pat nine. If this does not seem quite tight enough, we could screw it down to a one-card 7-5, or a pat 9-7. Perhaps the optimum would be to use the looser standard in a game with antes, and the tighter one with blinds only. Some super-tights wait for a one-card six or a pat eight; they do a lot of waiting, and get charged every deal.

In late position, you need to loosen up a lot. By the time there are only a couple of people yet to act behind you, garbage such as a good two-card draw or a pat jack does not smell bad at all. Much depends on who those two players are who still can whomp you.

The amount of a player's bet or raise tells a lot about that person's hand at no-limit lowball. A pat hand is much more likely to be a 9 or 8 than a better holding, and a pat six is hard to get. A player with a pat 9 or 8 is not enthusiastic about getting involved with guessing games after the draw against a one-card draw. He would rather end matters right away. Therefore, he tends to open for a greater amount of money than would a one-card draw, and his raises often overbet the pot by a wide margin. A big bet before the draw will be a passable hand, but not usually a monster.

Even though a big raise does not show a whopper, it will still normally be a pat hand. A one-card draw such as 7-4-3-A has no business calling such a raise. A good guideline to follow would be to fold unless these conditions are met: you have an excellent draw such as a six-joker, and there is a sizable amount of money yet to be bet (so you can make money after the draw, or run a bluff).

The "betting dialogue" between a one-card draw and a pat hand after the draw is a much more cut-and-dried conversation than in most poker situations. If the pat hand is first, he checks. To bet would be a strange play. If the opponent hits, he will have a good hand and bet himself (unless he has hit specifically an eight, where his play is unclear and depends on a number of factors). If the opponent misses, it is absolutely pointless to bet, as he won't call.

Some weaker players make the error of betting pat hands after the draw in this situation, on the theory of, "I really have a pat hand, and am not snowing." (To snow means to stand pat on a bluff). Snowing should be a rare play; it is used only very sparingly by good players. You are not likely to get called on suspicion by a one-card draw that busted out (you might have him beaten by accident, if he paired). All a bet does is jeopardize money for no return. If the hand is that rare creature good enough to hope for a call by a one-card draw that hit, why would you ever telegraph the fact and discourage a bluff?

If the one-card draw acts first, the play is also straight-forward. If he hits a good hand, he bets it. To check would be idiotic, as the pat hand is a big favorite to simply show his hand down. Betting into a pat hand after missing your draw is a common maneuver in lowball, so a bet there is subject to get called at any time.

You can see that a one-card draw against a pat hand figures to make the same amount of money whether it acts first or second, assuming the opponent has enough sense to check if he has to act first. This holds true whether the draw hits or bluffs. Therefore, position is not a major consideration for a one-card draw who is deciding whether to call a raise before the draw. The position is only helpful if the opponent turns out to be drawing a card himself, which would be unusual (for most players).

On the other hand, if you have a pat hand and get raised before the draw, position is highly valuable. You get to see whether an opponent draws, you might force him to act without prior information if he is unclear about whether to draw to a holding such as a pat 9-6 or 8-5, and your failure to reraise still leaves you with an unlimited hand. (Smooth-calling with a pat monster can work out well for you, and your opponent must consider this as a possibility).

The most frequent matchup at lowball will be between a couple of one-card draws. When you are first to act after the draw, do as follows:

(1) If you hit, vary your game by sometimes checking and more often betting.

(2) If you miss by catching a nearly hopeless card such as a 7 or 6 that pairs, bluff unless there is a good reason not to, such as feeling the opponent hit, or being against a habitual caller.

(3) If you catch an in-between card, check, and guess what to do if the opponent bets. Do not let the determining factor on whether to call be what you hit. If your opponent is a rational player, whether you have a king or a ten for low will not matter. You will either be way in front or way behind at the showdown. It is better to work at developing a good bluff-detecting nose.

In most games, a normal-size bet after the draw will be somewhere between two-thirds of the pot and the full pot. When bluffing, simply make a normal-size bet for the game you are in. Some people foolishly tend to make a smaller bet when having a legitimate hand (hoping to induce a call) and a larger bet when bluffing (hoping to induce a fold). Obviously, it is worth your while to pick up on this type of tell.

My experience is to be very wary about calling at the end when a one-card draw overbets the pot. Though it of course depends on who does it and when, your opponent is likely to show you a smooth six or a wheel. Don't be afraid to muck a seven if your nose tells you it's right.

A lot of play in lowball revolves around eight-lows. They are the rough equivalent of two pair in a high game; an in-between hand that is difficult to play properly, even for good players. Therefore, the fewer eights you build, the fewer problems you'll have. I don't draw to an eight when someone else opens unless it is a an aggressive player in steal position. Most eights you hit should be from hands where you opened the pot in late position in sort of a semi-steal, and got called (or by hitting an 8 in the draw).

The worst thing you can do when hitting eights after the draw is habitually use them for your check-and-call hand. Then you are following the cards instead of your nose. There is nothing wrong with betting an eight at no-limit lowball. Remember, you will only have such a hand when a policeman apprehended your attempted ante-steal. He may still put you on a steal after the draw.

Some players like to make a small-size bet when they make an eight. They also make the same size bet when stealing. This is bad poker. No matter which hand they hold for this dainty bet, a thunderously large raise rapes them. Even if they also make this size bet with a monster (not getting full value), monsters are hard to get. The big raise is an overwhelming favorite to be against a hand that can't call.

Another reason to make your bets with an eight close to the size of the pot is the policeman who doesn't know your game too well may be more likely to call on a bluff-catcher (bad eight, or a nine). He may put you on an inferior draw and figure there is no hand you could have hit that was worth that large a bet.

A pat eight is a good hand, but a dangerous one. If you open and get raised, you need about a pat 8-5 to play back, depending of course on who it is and how deep the money. If you reraise an opening raiser and he or someone else plays back at you, this means serious trouble. Be sure to distinguish between a play-back that puts you (or the opponent) all-in, and one that still leaves a sizable number of chips to be bet. A reraise that is all-in may be a player who has simply decided to "go with his hand." A reraise that still leaves a lot of chips is almost always a powerhouse.

Although we have been talking about Ace-to-Five lowball, Deuce-to-Seven lowball is not that much different, except for the obvious difference in hand-values. Here are a few pointers on playing "Deuce."

(1) The hand-values need adjustment as follows: The ace is only a high card at Deuce, but you need to adjust by more than one level, because of the lack of a joker, and the ruie about straights and flushes ruining a Deuce hand. A pat 9-8 at Deuce is markedly better than a pat 8-7 at Ace-to-Five. It is more like a pat 8-5.

(2) At Deuce, a one-card draw that makes a gutshot straight, such as 8-6-5-4, is much worse than it looks, and an open-ended straight is practically unplayable.

(3) A draw in Deuce can never be all that good, because there is no joker. A reraise is a virtual lock to be a pat hand of some sort. Seldom call a reraise if you are drawing.

No-limit lowball is an attractive form of poker, both for enjoyment and profit. Perhaps more than in any other form of poker, the person who is a good psychologist and reader of opponents has a nice edge that will get the cheese.

23-LOWBALL DRAW QUIZ
by Bob Ciaffone

The following problems take place at no-limit ace-to-five lowball with a joker. The game is eight-handed with a $10 ante, blinds of $15 and $25, and a minimum bring-in of $50. Assume that each player starts with $1,000 worth of chips. Problems one through six take place before the draw, and problems seven through twelve after the draw.

(1) You hold 9-8-7-4-2 under-the-gun. What do you do?

Answer —   fold (10)   raise (6)   call (2)

Explanation — Limit players open these rough nines with regularity. I think at no-limit a fold is in order. Your position is bad. The hand has no flexibility; you must stay pat. Someone else likely has the joker. This type of hand will not win a big pot, but can lose one if you get stubborn. The main function of a pat rough nine at no-limit is to steal the antes, which you should not be trying to do from an early position. Muck this dog.

(2) You hold 8-5-4-2-Joker. You open for $150 in early position and the button raises to make it $500 straight. What do you do?

Answer —   raise (10)   call (8)   fold (0)

Explanation — You have a through ticket even against a tight player. If you get a smooth eight cracked, there is no way to avoid losing all your chips. Against most players it is correct to raise all-in in case they are drawing (even though this is unlikely). Against someone you are sure has a pat hand, there is a cute play to be considered of simply calling. The main purpose of this is to discourage the opponent from breaking a loser such as 9-8-3-2-A or 8-7-4-2-A and drawing to beat you. Perhaps he will be confused when you simply call, and will stand pat. Nearly all the time I would simply play back and stand pat, but this cute play of just calling is worth mentioning.

(3) You open for $150 in early position on 9-7-5-2-A, and the button raises to $500 straight. What do you do?

Answer —   fold (10)   call (3)   raise (3)

Explanation — This hand has poor prospects. It is too weak a holding to stand pat, yet paying half your stack to draw out-of-position to 7-5-2-A is unsound poker. Therefore, you must fold.

(4) You are in the big blind with 7-7-4-2-Joker. The button opens for $150. What do you do?

Answer —   raise (10)   call (5)   fold (0)

Explanation — The button player may be trying to steal on a relatively weak hand. You have a high-quality one-card draw. I would raise to $500 or so and test my opponent. This situation where there are only a few players remaining to contend the pot is a place for reraising without a pat hand. Even if the opponent has a good hand you are not without chances.

(5) You open for $150 in early position holding 8-6-3-2-A. Everyone folds around to the big blind, who raises to $500 straight. What do you do?

Answer —   call (10)   raise (8)   fold (2)

Explanation - Again, you have to decide whether to raise all your chips in case the opponent is drawing, or call and entice him into standing pat with a loser. Here I believe the superior play is to call. The large amount of the raise indicates a pat hand, and it will be hard for your opponent to save his remaining $400 on the final betting round, as there is already about $1,300 in the pot. Of course, you might not have a winner, but that risk must be taken.

(6) You are on the button holding 3-2-A-A-A. A player in early position opens for $125 and a player in middle position calls. What do you do?

Answer — fold (10) raise (4) call (0)

Explanation — A two-card draw is unsound, even on the button, against opponents who will either be drawing one card or standing pat. While it may tempt some to try making a big raise and standing pat if called, because you hold so many low cards, I think this is a bit too exotic. There is another ace and the joker to be accounted for. Even without these cards, your opponents can make a six low. Their actions to this point indicate they have good hands. You have a bad hand, and are advised to fold it.

(7) You hold a one-card draw to a 7-6-3-2. You have opened in middle position for $125 and the button has called. What is your game plan after the draw if you pair?

Answer — bet if pairing the 7 or 6,
check if pairing the 3 or 2 (10)

bet if pairing any card (5)

check if pairing any card (0)

Explanation — It depends which card you pair. My advice against a random opponent is to run a bluff if you pair a non-wheel card; i.e. any card larger than a five. There is $355 in the pot. If I bet, whether holding a seven low or a pair of sevens or sixes, it feels right to bet about $300 in most games. If you bet on any pair you will be bluffing too often, according to game theory. Never bluffing means you don't understand the game.

(8) You have opened the pot in middle position for $150 and gotten one caller behind you. Each of you has drawn one card. You hit inside and make a 7-5-4-Joker-A. You decide to bet $325. The opponent moves you in for $525 more. Do you call or fold?

Answer —   fold (10)   call (3)

Explanation — There are only two possibilities against a rational and experienced player. Either he has you beaten, or he is bluffing. This type of raise is almost never made on a rough seven. Unless my table feel made me think the opponent was bluffing, I would fold. A raise after the draw at no-limit is going to be made normally on at least a six low.

(9) The opponent opens in early position for $125 and you call in late position. You each draw one card. You make a seven perfect (7-4-3-2-A) the opponent bets his entire stack of $875 into a $370 pot. What's going on?

Answer —   fold (10)   call (4)

Explanation — Once again, all you can beat is a bluff. Such a huge overbet of the pot size after the draw will not be made on a seven low. For most players, the main question is whether they are going to show you a six or a wheel. Since either of those hands beat yours, don't call unless you think the opponent is bluffing. It may seem strange to hit your hand and then fold when the opponent bets, but it sure looks right to do so here. And don't show the hand before folding, or you'll be bullied for the rest of the session.

(10) You are in the blind holding a great-looking pat 6-5-3-2-A. The button opens for $100, and you raise to $400, which he calls. He draws a card. What action do you take after the draw?

Answer —   check (10)   bet (3)

Explanation — Check this monster just like you would with any other pat hand. This gives you two shots. He may make a hand and bet, or he may decide to bluff. If you want a man to hang himself, leave some slack in the rope.

(11) You are in the blind with a pat of 8-6-4-3-Joker. An opponent opens in late position for $125, which you raise to $500 straight. He calls and stand pat behind you. Do you check, or bet your remaining $500?

Answer — bet (10)   check (3)

Explanation — Against most people I would bet the rest of my money. The odds say the opponent has a hand something close to what you're looking at. If he has a worse eight, he'll appreciate a free showdown. If he has you beat, it will be hard for you to get away from your hand, with over a grand in the pot and only $500 left. Against most players I would feel obligated to call if I checked and he bet. Therefore, I will bet myself.

(12) You pick up a pat 8-5-3-2-A. You open in early position for $150, and are called by the button and the big blind. Both opponents take one card. After the draw, the player in front of you leads out for $500. What do you do?

Answer — fold (10)   call (2)   raise (0)

Explanation — Even though you hold a well-above-average pat hand, you are between a rock and a hard place. Even if the bettor does not have you beat, he may run you into the nuts. The percentage play is to give up. A no-limit lowball player has to make some pretty big laydowns to play the game correctly.

Scoring: 120 = perfect
                      110-118 = very strong
                      100-109 = good player
                        90-99 = not bad
                        80-89 = need more study
                          0-79 = brings lots of money

24-LONDON LOWBALL
"Knowing The Odds Is Vital"

by Stewart Reuben

This game was first played at the Victoria Casino in London. It has spread out since then and is popular among those who enjoy fire-breathing poker. Each player antes £10 (it used to be £25) and receives two cards facedown and one faceup. The high card after the dealer must bet £25. The betting then goes around in the usual manner. A second card is dealt faceup, then a third, and then a fourth. Finally, a card is dealt facedown. There is a betting interval after each card, and the best low hand showing must lead off on each card after the first betting round. The best hand is 6 4 3 2 A (not 5 4 3 2 A), as both straights and flushes count high. Since an ace is used as a low card, a pair of aces is better than a pair of deuces.

Thus this is somewhat like the reverse of seven-card stud high, without the added color of the out-draw possibilities created by straights and flushes. London lowball is very similar to the game of "razz" as played in Las Vegas, but that is limit poker, and the straights and flushes have no significance.

The game, like five-card stud, has a limited strategy. It is extremely useful for this book as certain poker techniques can be explained with great clarity. In play, its great attraction is that it appears easy for weaker players to understand. Thus they don't feel at a disadvantage. Moreover, in my experience, people play horribly, and this is more discernible than in any other game.

This is a huge game. I wouldn't play in the game during its heyday, because frankly I couldn't afford to. I only joined in when they switched to half lowball, half Omaha. However, without making accounts, I suspect all my early winnings were at Omaha. This was due to the staking system, the amount of money with which people started, and the fact I played badly—particularly before starting to write this book.

Let us consider a ring game of eight players. The pot is £80. The highcard must bet £25. The first low card that wants to play raises £125 more. One other player calls and the high card passes. The pot is £405. Card four there is a bet of £400 which is called, total pot £1205. Card five the bet is £1200; card six £3600, and there could be a river bet of £10,800. These are heady sums, and hands were rare where players had enough money on the table for this to happen. More frequently a few people played with the minimum £1000. Then Player A makes the mandatory £25 bet. B raises and C calls. The pot is now £405. If D calls the pot will be £555. What is D to do if he started with only the minimum and wants to play? He may as well back-raise and get the agony over with. B or C may pass now or later, and thus D will gain some leverage for his money. The effect used to be that all the players banged in their money on third street or, at the latest, fourth street. The skill factor was relatively small. Since the table charge was £25 per hour, overall the loss rates to the house alone were substantial.

Nowadays the ante is only £10. Most people follow my example and don't raise the maximum at the start. In addition, few play with the minimum sum. On the other hand, the great attraction of the game, that mug punters were lured to it like moths to a candle, has sharply diminished because they have gone broke.

PRINCIPLES

(1) If you have a 10 or higher showing at card three and there are two or more players in the pot, you can pass blind. If you call, basically you must hit a valuable low card and all the others be dealt a turkey. The probability of each of you improving is about 50%. Thus you are 7-1 against catching both up. You are never given these odds. Even if it all comes to pass, you have only achieved a level playing field. Lowball is the only game I know where you can play perfectly passing blind.

(2) If the high card has bet and everybody else passed, you should raise blind with a low card. He is going to need two low cards in the hole even to consider calling, and that is 3-1 against. This rule does not apply where somebody is high with an 8 or lower, or possibly even a 9.

(3) Should you pass a raise if you were the high card with (4 A) K against (? ?) 7 ? If he is other than in a steal position, certainly. If he has made a mandatory raise, it is unclear. The problem is you may get sucked insidiously into a huge pot.

(4) Don't be frightened of letting a high card in, provided he must pay for the privilege. e.g. You raise small immediately after the high card with (7 3) 2. A player with a 10 calls. Now another low card raises. It is unnecessary to put the frighteners on the 10 by raising again. If he wants to play, basically the other low and you are splitting up his money. Of course, by all means reraise if you think the 10 will continue to come along for the full ride, but this would be really rare. Otherwise, the danger is he will hit a blank on fourth street and fail to throw all his lovely money away.

(5) Playing passively with a good low at the start and failing to raise is poor poker. It is too easy to be outdrawn. Just a small raise is all that is necessary.

(6) Card four: pass a hand such as (7 4) A J against (? ?) 5 7. If you call, you are hoping he has paired and the odds against this are 2-1. Even if you are correct, you are only a small favorite. Thus, London lowball conforms to the basic poker principle. **Always pass in a situation where you are a small favorite or big underdog.**

(7) (7 4) A 9 is more marginal against (? ?) 5 6. He may have paired, or if not, it is possible he has a four-straight. The holding of 2 3 5 6 isn't that big a deal against your hand.

(8) The decision whether to call with (3 2) 7 5 K against (? ?) 2 8 4 is a poker one. He can be expected have paired up about a third of the time. If he has taken a great deal of heat early on against two or more opponents and later hits an 8, it probably hasn't paired him.

(9) The rough 9 made (9-8 low) is a small underdog on fifth street against four cards to a 7.

(10) The holding 5 4 3 2 is an awful hand, because an ace or 6 make a worthless straight. A call constitutes a bluff. You can hit only an 8 or 7 for a decent low.

EXAMPLE 1

It is a sixhanded pot. The high card king bet £25. I with (3 2) A raised £50. Eva with (? ?) 2 called and Joe (? ?) 3 raised the pot. Both Eva and I called, so that the pot now stood at £1240.

Card four I had (3 2) A J, Eva (? ?) 2 Q and Joe (? ?) 3 Q. I bet £1240 which they both called.

Card five I held (3 2) A J J, Eva (? ?) 2 Q Q and Joe (? ?) 3 Q 7. Joe bet £4900, then having £4000 left. Both Eva and I passed.

Let us analyze this hand and the comments thereon. Poker players are always prepared to pontificate about a large pot. At card three my hand was exceptional, as I had one each of the low cards showing. It is diminished by the straightening possibility. Joe's raise can't be a bluff; there is nothing to bluff about. Personally, I wouldn't have escalated the pot in this way. Eva and I have already indicated our hands are playable.

Card four my hand is clearly best, but several commentated that it wasn't worth a bet. Bosh! Either player can hit seven cards on fifth street to make their hand totally useless. In addition, either could hit one of six cards to match one of their holecards. This would make the hand worthless unless both opponents bomb out. For all I know, Eva may have started with a hand such as (8 5) 2. This is perfectly valid, but an underdog to a potential 7 or 6. Note, I bet every penny of the pot. This is essential; my advantage is small and the odds must be made as unattractive as possible.

Disaster struck card five, when Joe seems to have the only playable hand. What is the probability that he had a 7 in the hole? Assuming he had a premium hand, i.e. three cards 7 or under, no worse than two to a middle-pin straight, and not holding 7 6 3; then he has a 7 in the hole 44% of the time. A really tight player will hold precisely 6 3 A. A looser one might hold an 8 in the hole, or a hand more likely to form a straight.

The probability that he has a 7 is 44%. Not that this could ever be worked out accurately at the table. But surely I am receiving 2-1 for my money and should have called? This is entirely fallacious. The odds aren't 2-1. The pot was £4960 and the bet £4900. However, there is no point in calling; I might as well raise the remaining £4000. Joe must call, even if he has paired up. Thus my true odds are:

(£9860 + 4000) / £8900 = 1.57 to 1. I need to win 40% of the time, not 33%. This is one of the most common errors in pot-limit poker; ignoring the fact that there's more money to be bet.

44% of the time I am a small favorite against Joe and 56% an enormous underdog. Even with a hand as marginal as (3 2) A J 10, matters are completely different. My jack low may stand up. With (3 2) A J 9, Joe is less likely to bluff if he has paired. Moreover, if Eva also didn't have a 7 in the hole, once I called she would realize the probability of Joe having paired up has increased. She might call as well, and I am no certainty against her hand.

Actually, Joe did have a 7 in the hole—which he showed with great glee. The only way I could have won the pot was either to play badly or to reraise on third street. Then there would have been no alternative to going all-in and I would have been favorite to win.

Note that the entire discussion about this hand concerned probability. Poker played no part in the analysis.

EXAMPLE 2

The following hand made the newspapers in England, as described by David Spanier's poker column in "The Independent."

I called at Card 3 on (8 2) A. All the other players showing high cards passed, as did one showing an 8 and two others with a deuce. Sid, also showing an ace, raised and I called. Sid was obviously already on heat.

Fourth Street Sid (? ?) A 3 and I held (8 2) A 5. Sid again bet the size of the pot. Few things give him greater pleasure than bluffing me out, but this time he was clearly charged up and had a big hand. Thus I put him on a 6 in the hole, most likely together with a 4. Holding such a hand, he is normally better than a 2-1 favorite. But I felt I had value; the only low cards to have passed match my holecards. Also, we had a great deal of money left to bet, and I had a good idea of my opponent's hand.

Card five brought Sid a 10 and me a Queen. Possibly here I should have passed. After all, I am losing. But a 10 is easily beaten.

Card 6: I held (8 2) A 3 Q 9 and Sid (6 4) A 3 10 3. I was now able to move in on him and set him in for the pot of £8000. We had just the right amount in front of us. I don't want him to have any betting money at the river. Sid called, hit a 7 and won the hand. Should I have passed, virtually having seen his holecards? I'll leave it to you to decide. It partly depends on how you want to play poker.

EXAMPLE 3

Card three: Our old friend Joe, high with a jack, bet the forced £25. Everybody passed to me, and I with (6 A) 4 raised £200. He called; we will forget the irrelevant holdings of the other players.

Card four; Joe showed (? ?) J 8 and I had (6 A) 4 6. I bet £500 and Joe called. I am quite certain this is a serious error; the 8 is too high a card. The pot now stood at £1600.

Card five; Joe had (? ?) J 8 3. I showed (6 A) 4 6 10. I bet £1200. Probably this is a mistake, but Joe must pass if he has paired up, and good things can happen next card. Joe now had £3000 left. By not betting the full pot-size each time, I had left myself room to maneuver.

Card six; Joe (? ?) J 8 3 3. I held (6 A) 4 6 10 6. Joe checked and so did I. There was no doubt in my mind, having called on fifth street, there was no way Joe was going to release now, and he was a big favorite. Joe shrugged his shoulders. Note that he has blundered. He intended to call, so he should have preempted me and gone all-in. I have virtually told him absolutely that I cannot beat a jack low. My hand cannot possibly be good enough to cleverly give him a free card.

Card seven Joe checked. I had (6 A 5) 4 6 10 6, having caught a 5 on the last card to make my 10-low. I bet the £3000 and he called. Thus I won a nice pot. As I raked in the chips, people muttered, "How could Stewart bet; Joe obviously had to be drawing to an 8-low." But I had a cast-iron winner. Joe would not check any 9 low or better on the end, precisely **because** it seems there is no chance whatsoever that I will bet.

Here we have entered into game theory. How can I give away such a valuable secret, just for the price of our book? Well, first of all, it is a very rare occurrence, e.g. the last bet must set Joe in. I cannot bet, in case he is sandbagging. Secondly, if I know you have read this, it changes everything. Now Joe can check blind, because a 10 7 or better would bet. We have transcended simple logic and are playing pure poker.

Don't overlook the fact that from card six I had a tremendous advantage, being last to act. If I had hit a picture instead of pairing, my hand would have been garbage.

EXAMPLE 4

This is the most common odds situation in lowball. To decide what is the correct play, we will need to know not only the odds, but also the amount of money left to be wagered. We will also have to use game theory to reach our conclusions. This is a heady mixture when most decisions are made in less than five seconds! We will play double-dummy and reveal the holecards. Bear with this analysis, as it reveals a great deal about all poker games where a card or cards are later dealt sight unseen to the players.

Al, a very tight strong player, after five cards shows (4 A) 5 6 K. Ted, of similar disposition, has (3 2) 7 8 9. They are playing heads-up. Ted is leading at the moment, with two cards to come. Al has a nice draw, and is actually a tiny favorite to win the pot if those last two cards are simply dealt out at this point with no further betting. An examination of what happens with money left to bet reveals a highly interesting situation. Ted can charge his opponent a price on each card if he wishes. However, the energy of the situation lies with Al, who can lash out with a large bet and confront Ted with an unpleasant guess to make: did Al hit, or is he bluffing?

How should the betting go? I don't know. You must tell me more, as the amount of money left for betting as compared to the pot-size is critical to the decision. Suppose there is £1000 in the pot.

1) With less than £2000 each left for wagering, Ted should bet. Ted is either a big favorite or a small dog. If Al has a pair, he will pass. Al could be paired, as he is a good enough player to have bluffed fourth street. If Al is not paired, as here, he should raise all-in. Then Al is about 11-10 favorite.

2) With £8,500 each left for wagering, Ted should bet £500, in case Al has paired. Al should call. If Al incorrectly raises at this point, then Ted can adopt the strategy of simply calling the raise, and then setting Al all-in on sixth street if he hits a bad card, thus depriving the draw of any betting leverage on the end.

Al's best play fifth street facing a £500 bet is to just call, for another reason. Many players (incorrectly) think it is proper to raise in this type of situation. When the big draw checks, the made hand may erroneously conclude that the draw has four cards to only a relatively mediocre low.

It is probably not so good for Ted to bet the full £1000. If he does this, Al can raise £3000. There is now £9000 in the pot and each player has only £4500 left. If Al hits a blank, it will cost him only £3000 to call. He will have 3-1 for his money, good odds even if Ted improves.

3) With very deep money, it is more dangerous for Ted to make that small bet (in case Al has paired). If Al has not paired, he should raise, because he is the real favorite, and has leverage on the end to boot. This differs from the preceding situation because here Ted is unable to reraise all-in. There will still be money left for Al to bet on the end if he wishes. With the money this deep, where Ted is in trouble making even a small probing bet, it is likely that Ted erred by playing his hand originally.

Let us suppose it is now sixth street, and both players have failed to improve. Ted shows (3 2) 7 8 9 10, and Al (4 A) 5 6 K Q. Assume there is now £2000 in the pot.

(1) With less than about £4000 left for wagering, the play is routine. Ted, who is now a solid favorite to win the pot with but one card to come, should bet, and Al should call.

(2) With a sum such as £8000 left for wagering, the situation is quite complex. But whether Ted bets or checks actually makes little difference to his long-run expectation. If Ted bets, Al will call. If Ted checks and Al incorrectly bets, Ted should raise all-in, as he is depriving the drawing hand of having any betting leverage if the hand is improved.

Here is the explanation why Ted's long-run expectation is about the same whether he checks or bets. Al will win on the river if he hits a 2, 3, 7, or 8. He will also win with a 9, provided his opponent does not help on the last card. Even though Al's chances to win the pot are less than Ted's, the leverage Al has from being able to bet on the end will just about cancel this out, in our example. (Should Ted's hand be worse than shown here, he should check; if better, he should bet.) For a mathematical analysis of this situation to demonstrate these statements, see the next chapter, "Important Pot-limit Concepts."

With Ted's situation on sixth street I generally bet a 9 low, and always check a 10-8 low in the same position. I have followed this plan twice with a mediocre 10 against an apparent 7-draw. In both cases, my opponent chose to bet with the visibly weaker hand, but apparently stronger draw. I then raised all-in, and each time they now passed! My apparent weakness had elicited a bluff.

(3) If on sixth street both players have a great deal of money left, Ted can now bet £500, and of course with his actual hand Al will call. Ted's bet makes certain Al doesn't get a free card if he has only four to a 9 low.

After all the cards are out, Ted should always check. Al should bet if he improves, plus bluff sometimes. Ted has an unpleasant guess to make whether to call. If Al bets only if he improves, Ted should always pass. If Al always bets, Ted should always call. In my experience, Al bluffs somewhat more than is justified, and Ted calls more readily than is demanded by the cards. Both players are trying to use game theory, which tells us how often a bluff should be run if both players play with mathematical correctness.

You may care to try this exercise. If Al guarantees he will bet if he improves or hits a J or Q, then it doesn't matter whether Ted calls or passes! If the pot is £2000, then Al wins £1200 of every pot played, and Ted £800. If Ted bets £2000 on sixth street, then Al calls. He then plays the river the same way, and still comes out about £1200 ahead each time.

Thus, it is totally marginal whether Ted bets or checks sixth street. If you gave Ted (4 3) A 8 9 10 and Al (7 2) 5 6 K Q, then Ted wins whenever they both hit an 8 low. This demonstrates how important it is to consider your second-highest card early in the pot.

Ted can try to beat Al's game theory ratio of bluffing with seven bad cards by refining his calling system. He might call only if he hits a card lower than a ten. Either he improves to an 8-low, or hits a blocker Al may have liked. Of course, if Al detects that Ted intends this, he can bluff more frequently. Certainly I have used such strategies against strong opponents, where it is a waste of time trying to read them.

Don't fall into the error I have seen any number of times. In the above situation after all the cards have been dealt, Ted foolishly bets all-in. After Al calls and shows down the winning hand, Ted says sheepishly, " I would have had to call anyway, so I might as well bet." Nod encouragingly. He has deprived the draw of the opportunity to bluff, and can be called only if he is losing.

This analysis shows us why pot limit is more intricate than limit. It also demonstrates why the game is usually played less rapidly.

For a more detailed analysis of the ideas presented in the discussion of this hand, please see the following chapter, "Key Pot Limit Concepts."

25-KEY POT-LIMIT CONCEPTS
by Bob And Stewart

London lowball is an excellent game for studying mathematical models that illustrate key principles of pot-limit play. The reasons are the last card dealt to each player is not visible to the others (as opposed to games with common cards like hold'em and Omaha), and it can be clear with one card to come that a hand is presently behind, but will certainly win if it improves. We will look at two related ideas in action. First, proper bluffing frequency; second, the leverage on the end that a drawing hand possesses.

How often should a drawing hand bluff if it busts out? Naturally, this is a decision with strong psychological elements. But we should be aware that mathematics can dictate the proper frequency if those elements are removed, and the participants in the pot play in a "correct" manner. By "correct" we mean at random and with the proper frequency of calling and folding.

Game theory says to determine the proper frequency of bluffing, we should make the decisions on the last betting round of either always calling or always folding yield the same result. We do this by bluffing exactly half as often as the frequency of betting with a winning hand. Then it will not matter in the long run how the opponent reacts to our bet. He will get the same result.

Let us use a concrete example to illustrate this principle. Suppose there is a grand in the pot going into seventh street. Player A has the best hand right now, and player B will have the best hand in all cases where he improves on the last card. At the river player A should of course check. Suppose player B has ten winning cards he can hit. If B bluffs on five of the cards where he misses, then B is bluffing the precise amount that no matter what strategy player A adopts, the outcome will always be the same. If A always folds, he will not lose any additional money. If A always calls, he will lose $10,000 on the hands where B has hit, but gain back $10,000 on the five hands where B has run a bluff ($5,000 in B's bluffs, plus another $5,000 that was originally in the pot). Another way to look at the situation is that when player B bets on the end using the proper game strategy of bluffing half as often as having the goods, then Player A getting 2-1 on the money will break even by always calling. Note that B is doing well on these fifteen hands despite bluffing, profiting by winning an equivalent amount to the main pot. A good player is going to do better than in our mathematical model. He will vary from the dictates of game theory by noticing whether his opponent is normally a caller or a folder, whether he has a tell when bluffing, and so forth.

Here is another model, to tell us when the player with the best made hand should check going into the last card to deprive the opponent of the extra leverage gained from the bigger pot size.

Suppose two players are contesting a pot with a grand in it. As previously, Player A is leading with one card to come, and Player B is trying to draw out. Assume there is enough money left for a bet and raise, or a bet now and a bet on the end. For a grand in the pot, this amount would be four thousand apiece. How much the best of it does Player A need to have for it to be correct to bet at the point there is one card to come? Remember, the bet now triples the amount that B can bet on the end. Is betting a good idea when you are increasing the leverage for the drawing hand on the end?

Let us look at where the break-even point between betting and checking is located. That point is when B has exactly a third of the available cards with which to improve. We illustrate this by seeing what happens in our thousand dollar pot when there are 30 unknown cards, B draws out with 10 of them, and A has his hand stand up with the other 20. (For most games, there would be more unknown cards than this, but the ratios are the same, and these numbers are easier to work with.)

B will bet on his 10 winning cards, and 5 of his losing cards. In the case where A checks with one card to come, and always calls on the end (note that always folding yields the same result), A is going to break even on his action. A makes a profit of $2,000 x 5 = $10,000 on the five hands where B bluffs, plus $1,000 x 15 = $15,000 on the fifteen hands where B busts out and does not attempt to bluff. Thus A shows a total profit of $25,000 on all the pots that he wins. On the ten pots that A loses, he is out 10 x $1,000 = $10,000. Thus, we see that A, by checking with one card to come, will win $15,000 on the long-term average, according to game theory. B will win $2,000 for each hand he completes and lose $1,000 for each hand he loses. Thus, he also wins $15,000. The total $30,000 is the original money in the pot on Card Six.

How does A do by betting the pot with one card to come? Assume that B calls the $1,000 bet at this point, and that A calls B's $3,000 bet on the end (as we know, folding on the end yields the identical result). Player A will make a profit of $5,000 x 5 = $25,000 on the five pots where B bluffs, plus $2,000 x 15 = $30,000 on the fifteen pots where B does not bluff. Thus A shows a total profit of $55,000 on all the pots that he wins. On the ten pots that A loses, he is out 10 x $4,000. So by betting with one card to come, Player A's profits are again $15,000.

The preceding discussion to prove our premise is quite involved, but the premise itself is easy to grasp. According to game theory, the break-even point between betting and checking in the situation we have outlined is when the drawing hand is a 2-1 underdog. If the leading hand is a greater than 2-1 favorite with one card to come, it is correct for him to bet. If the leading hand is less than a 2-1 favorite, it is correct for him to check. Note that when A checks, B must not bet, or A will reraise him all-in, which deprives B of any leverage on the end, leaving him a 2-1 dog as a result.

We should mention the cases when A definitely should bet, to make everything crystal clear. Anytime you are the favorite and have the best hand, be sure to bet if you can thereby get the opponent all-in before the last card. Now the drawing hand does not have any implied odds, and the made hand extracts the maximum from the situation. Second, do not try to apply this mathematical principle to games where the last card is dealt faceup, giving the made hand important information about when to call and when to fold should the drawing hand bet on the end. The drawing hand normally has less leverage in such a situation.

We should apply the information in our discussion to find out how big an underdog the drawing hand must be to fold when the opponent bets the pot with one card to come. He does not have to go strictly by the pot odds, as the implied odds help him because of his betting leverage on the end. When the opponent bets the size of the pot, you are getting 2-1 on the money for a call. So if you can bring your implied odds up to make you no more than a 2-1 underdog, you should call. As we have seen, the implied odds say the power of the drawing hand enhances the actual odds by a factor of fifty percent. So a player with a two-ninths chance to win the pot is actually a three-ninths contender for the money. Three-ninths chance is the same as saying a 2-1 underdog. This means any time the drawing hand has two chances out of nine to win the pot, it is correct to call a pot-size bet. As we have said, this applies only when the draw can bet the size of the pot on the end.

So the important pot-limit concepts presented in this section are:

(1) On the end a drawing hand should bluff half as often as it bets with a winning hand, assuming the opponent is playing correctly according to game theory.

(2) The earning power of a drawing hand is increased by fifty percent by being able to bet on the end. This means:

(a) Any time the made hand is a favorite, he should make the drawing hand go all-in when he can do so.

(b) With one card to come, if the made hand cannot get the drawing hand all-in (or close to it), the made hand should bet only when he is at least a 2-1 favorite.

(c) With one card to come, the drawing hand should call any time he is no worse than a 7-2 underdog, provided he has the option of a pot-size bet on the end.

The same analysis cannot be applied as rigorously to no-limit. Suffice to say, if you intend to bluff by over-betting the pot, and want to play according to game theory, then you should bluff less frequently.

26-LONDON LOWBALL QUIZ
by Stewart Reuben

1. The High Card (? ?) K has brought it in. Everybody has passed.
You have (7 7) 7. What should you do?
Raise (2). Call (-5). Pass (0).
If you're worried about raising, just raise $600. Note he needs two
cards 7 or better to call and that's 3-1 against. You are getting even
money for your action.

2. Before you can act, one low card has called, a second raised, a
third called and a fourth raised. You have A 2 8. What should you
do: (a) with the 8 showing   (b) with the 8 concealed.
Pass (2) Call (-1) Raise (-5).
No matter how live your potential cards, there is going to be a raise
and you'll end up all-in against people drawing better than you. It is
too late for the fact that the 8 is concealed to make any difference.

3. King brings it in. 2 calls. 6 raises. A calls. 6 raises. 4 raises.
You hold (A 6) 2.
Raise the maximum (2). A small raise (1). Call (1). Pass (0).
The time has passed for fancy play. All the money is going in and
you have the ultimate hand—but don't be surprised if you lose.
Passing isn't so dreadful, provided you are extremely tight and want
to pick a better spot. But don't tell anyone after the pot.

4. (? ?) 7 2 has bet. (? ?) 3 8 calls. You hold (A 4) 7 9.
Pass (2). Call (-2). Raise (-100).
The second player at least is certainly beating you.

5. You hold (6 5) 2 3. Two players are to speak with (? ?) A 8 and
(? ?) 7 2.
Check (2). Bet (1).
You aren't giving away all that much as a 4 is ruination. Marvelous
things may happen if you hit an ace later. Unhappily, if you bet and
the A 8 calls, the 7 2 may raise.

6. (? ?) 6 5 has bet. (? ?) 3 Q calls. You hold (A 2) 4 7.
Raise the same amount as the first player (3). Raise the pot (2).
Call (-1). Pass (-100).
If the first player cooperates, he will also raise a small tempter. If
the Q again calls, it is time to move in. This is a rare example of
two players cooperating legitimately. Very few lowball hands are
worth slowplaying on fourth street; the 3 Q can catch up. Thus a
call is mediocre. Oddly enough, if the middle player holds (? ?) 3 8,
often a small raise will budge him whereas he will keep coming for
a monster bet. This is because he doesn't fancy bruising his ego
during the agony of a series of small raises.

7. (3 2) 7 5 9 against (? ?) 3 6 A facing (a) an all-in bet (b) a pot
bet where there are still bundles left to bet. He has charged on third
and fourth streets.
Call (2) Pass (1). Raise (in the latter case) (-10).
He may well have paired up. Next card you should pass if he hits a
good card, possibly even if you do so as well.

8. (A 2) 6 6 against (? ?) 3 K which has checked.
Bet small, e.g. $200 (2). Bet the pot (-2). Check (1).
Provided both of you have lots of money left, you have the
advantage because he will always be first to speak and it is more
difficult for him to hit a 6. Also people start acting a little crazy
when they see you bet with the "inferior" hand.

9. (A 4 5) 8 3 9 7 against (? ? ?) 7 6 6 Q, where you have bet sixth
street.
Check (2). Bet (0).
In the heat of the battle your opponent has forgotten you may well
have a better four to a 7 than him. A small bet may jog his memory.
You must leave him room to bluff.

10. A K Q J 10 suited and 6 4 3 2 A are both known as Royals.
What is the probability of hitting each in five cards?
Royal Flush 650,000 to 1 (2). Royal Low 2530 to 1 (2).

Because they are both called Royals, people think a perfect low is much more improbable than it actually is.

I (SR) worked with my friend David Levy of Intelligent Games Ltd. on computers to play poker. The very first sample random hand he sat down to play against the machine was hold'em, and that was the first hand he had ever played of this particular version of poker. The flop was K♥-J♥-10♥ and he had A♥-Q♥. Of course, he slowplayed with a check on the flop and fourth street after the machine had checked. Finally, he bet on the river and the machine passed. Now, that is what I call an ultimate bad beat!

Score	Comment
23-27	Find yourself another game from ours
16-22	You should be a winning player
10-15	Nobody wets their lips in anticipation when you play
0-9	Reread this book before risking your money
Under 0	Would you like to play some poker?

27-HIGH-LOW SPLIT
"Aim for the whole pot"

by Bob Ciaffone

High-low split is an increasingly popular form of poker. Nowadays, it is almost exclusively played with a qualifier of eight-or-better for low. A no-qualifier game makes the strategy very simple; play for low. A qualifier puts balance into the game.

Most split-pot games are played at limit poker. However, pot-limit high-low split is not only playable; it is an interesting, challenging, and intricate form of poker. For pot-limit it is better to play cards speak rather than having the players declare their direction. A declare increases the ease and profitability of collusion.

Although it is possible to play any form of poker with a pot-limit eight-or-better format, some games are more suitable than others. Omaha, both the regular and the five-card variety, is ideal. Hold'em is not good, since you can seldom play a hand without an ace in it.

For seven-card stud, it is advisable to deal four cards to each player (two down, two up) before the initial betting round. This will reduce the number of betting rounds from five to four, thus keeping stud in balance with the other games in the amount of monetary fluctuation. It will also bring flushes and straights into the picture better.

Draw poker is okay, although some prefer to introduce a third betting round through the use of a spit-card. This is a community boardcard turned up after the first betting round and before the players draw cards. Another game fun to play high-low is California pineapple. Each player gets dealt three cards, and must throw away one after the flop. At the end you may play either one or two cards from your hand. The board is the same layout as in hold'em. This game is identical to the British Isles game of "Three-card Irish," except you are not allowed to play the board.

Since there are so many forms of poker that can be played pot-limit eight-or-better, it would be too big a task to discuss them individually. Rather, let us talk about the general principles that pertain to all the various kinds of poker that use this format.

At pot-limit you seldom see the fivehanded and sixhanded pots that often characterize limit eight-or-better poker. Most pots are either played heads-up or threeway. This means if you split the pot, your profit is small in proportion to the amount of money risked. In order to make a good score, you must do the following:

(1) Play only very high-quality hands. The starting requirements for eight-or-better are more stringent than for high poker. In particular, you must avoid the flaw of trying to play every hand here that you would play at straight high. Look at it this way; if you play all the hands you would normally play for high, and also play hands that look attractive for low, you will be playing about **twice** as many hands as you would play in straight high. You should actually be playing somewhat **fewer** hands, so this loose style of play is a cardinal sin.

(2) Stick to hands with scoop potential. The place to aim for this goal is in your selection of starting hands. For example, at Omaha the ace-deuce combination is desirable, because it aims at the nut low. But if your hand is A-9-8-2 of four different suits, its scoop potential is small. This hand is worth much more at limit play with those many-handed pots than at pot-limit play. The next time you play it heads-up, make the nut low, and get quartered for big bucks, realize that you did something wrong and were not just unlucky. A hand such as A♥-K♠-Q♠-2♥ would have been much more valuable. The flush-draws help a lot.

There are two ways to scoop a pot. You can win both the high and the low, or you can win the high when there is no low. Anyone who claims that proper eight-or-better strategy is to play for low is horribly mistaken. He is still thinking in terms of the no-qualifier high-low split games which are not played anymore.

A hand that aims only at high is not a bad hand at all. But it must constantly be re-evaluated with each new card. For example, the Omaha hand of Q♦-Q♥-10♦-9♥ is a nice starting holding. With a flop of Q♠-J♥-3♣, it is a monster. A flop of Q♠-4♣-3♣ is only one card different and still makes you top set, but actually is a whole new ballgame. This second flop has two cards to a low, a flush-draw, and a card that makes the nut low-draw a straight. The first flop gives you a powerhouse, but the second gives you a trap hand that needs to take off a safe card before a large amount of money is committed. Only after an offsuit big card comes on fourth street, or the board pairs, should you go to war.

(3) Pot-limit eight-or-better is a game of position. Even though position is of great import in any form of big-bet poker, at eight-or-better it is of even more importance. You need position to see how the opponent reacts to the presence or absence of a possible qualifying low. Only then can you play your own holding at maximum effectiveness.

(4) Although there is bluffing, eight-or-better is not a bulldozer's game. You will find that a large number of bets are called. Even though the caller often has his heart in his mouth praying you are going the other way, he still puts the money into the pot. Eight-or-better is a game that places the accent on selecting good hands and reading situations well, rather than blowing away the opposition with a heavy betting hand.

(5) A pot-limit high-low split player needs a good sense of when to try and move someone out of the pot and when to leave them in. For threehanded pots, when you look like a lock in your direction but do not have a chance to scoop, you need to have someone in the middle—and keep them there. Quite often you do not want to apply maximum pressure in the betting, because you don't want to get the pot reduced to a heads-up situation. Of course, if winning your half of the pot is in jeopardy, try to remove the threat if possible.

The thought I will leave you with is that pot-limit poker is quite suitable to being played high-low, as well as one winner. If you like limit high-low poker, you will love it at pot-limit betting.

28-HIGH-LOW SPLIT QUIZ
by Bob Ciaffone

(1) At seven-card stud, you are dealt (K♠ Q♠) J♠. The lowcard makes a forced bet and a player with an ace showing makes a small raise. What do you do?

Answer —   fold (10)   call (0)   raise (-3)

Explanation — Muck this dog. Even if you catch a spade on fourth street, this would put you only at about even money, and probably for only half the pot.

(2) At seven-card stud, you make an eight low on fifth street with (A♣ 2♣) 5♥ 7♦ 8♣. Your right-hand opponent shows K♣ 9♦ 2♣ and bets the size of the pot. The player on your left shows Q♥ J♥ 7♣. All of you have plenty of money left. What is your action?

Answer —   call (10)   raise (4)   fold (-10)

Explanation — You appear to have a mortal lock on low. A scoop is extremely unlikely, as you would have to backdoor a high hand. It is important that there is extra money put into the pot for you to split with the player who wins high. If you raise, it certainly looks as though the player on your left will be forced to fold. Perhaps a simple call by you will allow him to continue in the pot, which of course is what you want. At seven-card stud, where a player's direction may be obvious, consider what would be the likely result if you raise when holding a lock. It is often better to not apply too much heat in a multi-handed pot. In addition, your opponents may draw an incorrect conclusion about your hand from your failure to raise.

(3) The game is five-card Omaha. You are on the button holding A♣-J♠-9♦-6♦-2♥. Two players limp in calling the blind. What do you do?

Answer — call (10) fold (4) raise (0)

Explanation — An A-2 combination is nice at high-low split, but the rest of the hand is quite junky. Your ace is not suited, and your back-up card for low is only a six. I prefer a call rather than a raise. Don't look for trouble. Frankly, Stewart prefers a fold.

(4) At four-card Omaha, you pick up an A♠-A♥-9♦-5♣ in first position. What is your action?

Answer — call (10) fold (9) raise (4)

Explanation — Do not attempt to narrow the field with a raise. Even though you prefer avoiding a multihanded pot, your hand is simply too weak to be shooting it up. Neither of your aces is suited, and A-5 is not likely to win low. Call the blind if you must, but if the pot gets raised behind you, get out.

(5) At Omaha, you are on the button with A♠-K♦-4♠-3♦. A couple of players in early position call the blind. What do you do?

Answer — raise (10) call (3) fold (-6)

Explanation — Your hand has good potential in both directions. A raise is in order. Don't reserve raises only for hands that have an A-A or A-2 combination.

(6) At Omaha, you pick up K♠-Q♥-J♣-10♥ in late position. The player under-the-gun opens for the minimum and the player in front of you makes a full-size raise. What do you do?

Answer —   call (10)   fold (7)   raise (0)

Explanation — This is a clear call. Even though you cannot win low, a good hand for high like this one can scoop the pot. The cards you need for high make it likely that if you hit help on the board, nobody will be able to qualify for low.

(7) At Omaha, you are dealt 10♠-9♥-8♠-7♥ in fairly early position. The player on your right opens by calling the blind. What do you do?

Answer —   fold (10)   call (3)   raise (-3)

Explanation — A typical high-low pot is threehanded, with one player going for high, another for low, and someone getting carved up in the middle. Obviously, high cards aim for high, and low cards aim for low. What does someone foolish enough to enter a pot with middle-sized cards like these aspire to? Don't be surprised if you wind up in the middle when playing such a hand.

(8) At Omaha, you hold in early position A♠-K♥-Q♦-J♣. The flop in a fivehanded pot comes A♣-A♦-Q♠, giving you a virtually unbeatable aces full. The first player checks and it's up to you. Do you check or bet?

Answer —   check (10)   bet (5)

Explanation — At limit poker you must charge a price to someone who might draw at a backdoor low. At pot-limit you can afford to check. If a low card comes on fourth street, someone who picks up a draw would still be erring by calling your pot-size bet. I think it is superior to check. Maybe someone will make a straight or a full house on fourth street with a free card, whereas they would have folded had you bet on the flop.

(9) In an Omaha game you pick up A♥-K♦-Q♣-3♦ in late position. Five of you stay for the flop, which is J♣-6♣-2♣, giving you a draw at the nut low. The first player comes out firing the size of the pot and the second player calls. What is your action?

Answer —   fold (10)   call (3)   raise (-2)

Explanation — Whenever you have a low draw with no chance for high, there is the risk of a tie for low. Tying with one other player means getting back 75 cents on each dollar you put into the pot. Tying with two other players means getting back 50 cents on the dollar. Here the most likely layout is the bettor has a flush and the caller the same low-draw as you. If this is actually so, it would be an error to play. A further drawback to your hand is if the low gets counterfeited on the end by an ace or three, you have no back-up low card and will get zero. I recommend folding this hand.

(10) At Omaha, you hold Q♦-J♥-J♣-10♥. The flop comes J♦-7♣-2♦, giving you top set. You bet the pot and get a call from the button. On fourth street comes the 6♣, making a low possible. You prudently check. The opponent bets the size of the pot. There is still plenty of money left. What now?

Answer —   fold (10)   call (5)   raise (0)

Explanation — Your opponent undoubtedly has made his low and is freerolling for high. Even though your three jacks are still the best possible high, they will almost surely be in jeopardy after fifth street is dealt. There are flushes working in two suits, and many cards could make a straight. Since there will be no good way to know whether your opponent has scooped or is still betting his low when he fires on the end, you will be faced with an unpleasant guess. Here is how the math works. Suppose there is now $100 in the pot and the opponent bets $100. You are simply trying to protect half the present pot ($50) if you call. By calling now and again on the river, $400 more will be put in jeopardy ($100 + $300 more on the end). This means you're laying 8 to 1 the opponent won't outdraw you. It is better to fold now than to try and protect that $50 by chasing with a big hunk of your stack.

You can see by the reasoning used in this quiz that the most important principle of pot-limit high-low split is to **aim for the whole pot**, both in your selection of starting hands and subsequent play. Without scoop potential, the amount of possible gain is small, but the amount of exposure is large. Go for **all** the gelt.

Scoring:
- 100 = perfect
- 92- 98 = very strong
- 86- 91 = good player
- 80- 85 = not bad
- 70- 79 = need more study
- 0- 69 = brings lots of money

29-STRIP DECK POKER
by Stewart Reuben

No, not strip poker, a game with completely different objectives from the normal game. This one is played with 32 cards, all the deuces through sixes are removed from the deck. It can be played either five card draw or five card stud, normally the latter.

Each player receives one card facedown and one faceup. The high card has to bet and there is a betting interval. Each player receives three more cards faceup, with a betting interval after each. One seemingly idiosyncratic rule is that a flush beats a full house. This is because it is much more difficult to get a flush when a stripped deck is used, as a suit consists of only eight cards. The sequence 10 9 8 7 Ace is a low straight, as an ace can still be used for a low card. In some remote places three of a kind does beat a straight, but usually a straight is considered the better hand. (If five cards are dealt out randomly there will be more straights than trips.)

I am glad to say this game is little-played now. It is excellent for cheating, as two players can easily communicate to each other what their hole card is. When there are only 20 unseen cards, this can be a big plus. In addition, it is easy to mark the cards, and the dealer can work out what card his "friend" would like to be given.

Actual odds can be calculated and the probability of making an inside straight can certainly be high enough to justify calling on fourth street. It used to be a big gambling game, appearing deceptively simple like London lowball.

A prime point is that you should **never** bet into a possible lock. e.g. You hold (A) K 10 8 A against (?) A 10 8 7. This starkly shows the distinction from limit. He could easily have been couping along and you calling. Now he checks at the river, or even bets. A bet or raise not all-in could be suicidal. He simply raises and you have no idea whatsoever what hole card he holds. This is basically the error Steve McQueen made against Edward G Robinson in the movie "The Cincinnati Kid."

I love the late Harry Rubin story. At a club he once ran, he was playing poker in a strip-deck draw game with a group of good customers. He opened in last seat with A♦-K♦ (a terrible holding). Several players called and he took three cards. After the draw there was a tremendous amount of action before it ever got to him, a bet and two raises. He looked at his hand and found he had struck gold; A♦-K♦-Q♦-J♦-10♦, a royal flush. He quickly mucked his hand. His reasoning? It was his club, he was dealing, and the customers might be suspicious he had cheated! A judicious pass might well be more financially rewarding in the long run.

30-TOURNAMENT STRATEGY
by Bob Ciaffone

Playing in pot-limit and no-limit money games does not completely prepare a person for tournament play. A formal competition has somewhat different strategy, and vastly different psychology. There are enough dissimilarities to fill a whole book. Some top tournament players actually have trouble breaking even in money games, and vice versa. Here are seven pointers for the big-bet poker player who wishes to enter a tournament.

First, the length of a tournament event has a great effect on the style of strategy used. Many events are one-day competitions. A satellite tournament usually lasts only about a couple of hours. The World Championship, a $10,000 buy-in no-limit hold'em contest held every spring, is a four-day event.

In a tournament, antes and blinds are raised on a regular basis. Competitors are eliminated as they run out of ammunition, and eventually the winner emerges, having won all the chips in play. The frequency with which the antes, blinds and betting structure are increased has a great influence over the pace of play. When the stakes are raised at rapid intervals, such as in a satellite event, aggressiveness becomes even more important. Often at hold'em or Omaha, no player will have a hand that has much of an advantage before the flop. For example, a pair of sixes has little edge at hold'em against two overcards such as a Q-J. Being the bettor and getting your money in first gives you three shots to win. The opponent may fold, you might have the best hand and have it hold up, or you can get lucky and draw out. One thing is for sure; in a pot-limit or no-limit hold'em satellite, the meek inherit little.

Second, position is usually worth less in tournament play. For most situations, the size of the antes and blinds in relation to the size of your stack is far greater in tournaments, especially those events of shorter duration. Hold'em and Omaha have four betting rounds, but in a tournament someone is often all-in well before the last card has been dealt. As we know, being able to exercise a positional advantage on all the betting rounds is preferable to having the betting end early because someone is all-in.

There is also something we players only half jokingly refer to as "The right of first bluff." This means the player who has to act first has the opportunity to launch a bluff before his opponent can do the same. Many pots come up in fastpaced tournament events where nobody has an even passable hand. Whoever bets first will win the pot. Is having to act before the opponent a disadvantage in such situations?

Third, the psychology of tournaments is substantially different from money play. Many money games become attractive because one or more players go on tilt. Many people become steamers after losing some big pots and getting stuck. They will call, bet, or raise in that circumstance on far more meager values than normal. In a tournament, losing a big pot usually means you are out of the competition. The player does his steaming from the rail, and you lose out on the benefit.

There are quite a few tournament players who do not seem to be playing for the purpose of winning prize-money. Rather, their goal is to see how long they can last "playing with the big boys." You should exploit this attitude in an opponent by bullying him with your chips, to put it bluntly.

A good player usually approaches tournament play with an entirely different attitude than the survivalist. If he is going to finish out of the money, he would prefer to bust out early. "Time equals money," as the saying goes, and there are often attractive cash games available for those who get eliminated.

Fourth, because the psychology of tournament play is so different from money games, many players will change their style of play in competitions. Some actually do a Jekyll and Hyde act, going from a loose plunger to a subdued sitter. Observe how each of your opponents is playing in the tournament, and pay more attention to this than how they usually play for money.

Fifth, most money games are played with blinds, whereas tournament competitions often use an ante in addition to the blinds. Use of an ante changes the play quite a bit. There is a lot more money in each pot at the start.

Getting your fair share or more of this booty is important. To do this, prefer to raise when you are the first person to enter a pot. If someone raises in front of you, he might be trying to rob the antes himself. This is especially likely if the game is shorthanded. If you have enough strength to call a raise, it may well be preferable to reraise instead. In fact, you may not even want to wait for a hand this strong to play back, if the situation is right.

Sixth, it is possible to be a winning money player without excelling at shorthanded play. You can simply quit a cash game when it gets short. This is not true for tournament play. Poker prize funds are structured to pay far more for the top spots. It is hard to get all the chips without beating the second-place finisher heads-up. And the only way to avoid playing shorthanded is to get eliminated from the competition. If you are to be a successful tournament player, it is an absolute must to become proficient at shorthanded play. See the discussion of satellite play later on in this section, and the chapter titled "Shorthanded Play," for some advice on how to do this.

Seventh, at the final table of a tournament, your chip position can have a powerful effect on your strategy. Can you win a bigger prize by staying out of the action until a short stack goes broke? Suppose most of the finalists have $5,000 to $20,000 in front of them. You have only $2,000, but there is one competitor who is in worse shape. He has only $400, which is the amount of the big blind. If the payoffs are structured so finishing in the next higher place puts you in the money or substantially increases your prize, try to stay out of pots and give the unfortunate one a chance to go broke.

If you have a lot of chips, play differently. That little guy who needs to rob the antes to stay alive is an excellent target. He may not have much of a hand, and losing to him is not fatal. The guy with a big stack is also vulnerable. Your little jabs can get him thinking about getting busted just when things looked rosy. But avoid playing a big pot against him unless you have a potent hand. The right play on a hand late in a tournament may be markedly different from the right play under normal conditions.

Since the amount of a player's chips have a profound effect on his play, it is obvious that in tournaments you must pay extra attention to the size of each stack around the table. For example, short stacks are much more common in tournaments than cash games. You'd be surprised how often during a tournament I have seen the foolish play of a bluff made when one of the players in the pot was all-in, or an opponent had so few chips left he had to call.

As you can see, being a skillful money player is no guarantee of success in tournament play. Especially at pot-limit, the character of play changes. You should look for opportunities to acquire tournament experience in small one-night weekly competitions, if these are available. Even if the betting structure is limit rather than pot-limit, you will gain insight into tournament strategy. You may even be starting on the road to a World Champion title someday.

In 1996 I wrote an article for "*The Card Player*" magazine on satellite tournament strategy, which is reprinted in the remainder of this chapter. This type of event calls for adjustments to be made in your game from the regular tournament strategy you employ, so I feel a discussion of these changes is worthwhile.

A satellite poker tournament is a contest to win an entry into a larger tournament. Most satellite tournaments are one-table events where first place is the only finishing position that receives a prize. Our discussion will confine itself to this type of satellite, as a multi-table satellite that pays several places is more like a regular tournament in nature.

Any time you change the scoring system for a game, it is necessary to make an adjustment in the strategies you use. Satellites are sufficiently different from a regular tournament event to require a rethinking of some of the methods employed.

Those of you who compete regularly at tournament poker are aware of how important it is to knock opponents out of the event when you have reached the final table. The reason this is important is that it is possible to win a prize, sometimes a pretty good-sized prize, by simple survival, without ever accumulating a large number of chips. This applies to any event that pays more than one place. Any time someone gets knocked out of the event, it improves your own chances, even if you did not get any of the chips.

A winner-take-all tournament is different. The only way you can get a prize is to "pay" for it with the chips you have won. It is important to realize that even though the last two or three players sometimes make a deal, this does not change the nature of a winner-take-all tournament. If there are three players left, and two of the players have nearly all the money, it is unlikely that a deal will be made, and the third player wouldn't get much if a deal was struck. Even a world champion is not going to intimidate his adversaries if he only has a couple of chips left.

To illustrate my point about the different strategy needed for a winner-take-all tournament, let me propose a hypothetical question. Suppose you are in a satellite tournament that started with ten players, each getting $300 worth of chips, so the total number of chips in play is three grand. (this is a common format for satellite play.) Through your devastatingly skillful play, you have amassed half the chips ($1500). My question is would you rather have the remaining $1500 all in the hands of one player, or divided among three other players, each with $500? Naturally, if the event paid more than one place, you would want only one other player, since this cinches second place for you. But here, second place pays zero. Is anything gained for you by having fewer players? No. I cannot see where it is any easier to beat one opponent out of fifteen hundred than three players out of five hundred apiece. So remember that your goal in a satellite event is to accumulate all the chips, not to outlast most of the other players.

Perhaps this is a timely moment to discuss the practice of a portion of the players at a one-table satellite to have a small pool of money taken up in a voluntary special collection and awarded for second place. Naturally, you must have kicked in to the collection to be eligible to win this pool money. Thus, it is quite possible that the person who actually finishes second in the satellite will not be involved in the pool, so the highest finish among the pool members will get the cheese.

The strategy for lasting the longest (yet not winning first place) is quite different than the strategy for amassing all the chips.

To survive, you avoid confrontations and risk-taking as much as you can, hoping for an obviously favorable situation before doing battle. A bluff is something to be avoided if possible. I believe that getting involved in a pool that rewards survivalist tactics reduces your chances of winning the satellite. Pool members give up a little something to non-pool members because they have an incentive to employ a less-than-optimum strategy for winning the satellite. A person who wants to be a successful competitor—it doesn't have to be at poker—should not be doing anything that causes him/her to lose focus on the primary task. Michael Jordan did not make a side bet with Scotty Pippen on who was going to score the most points in a Bull's game that night. Even a bet of an inconsequential amount like five bucks would be an unacceptable distraction.

The fact is many satellite entrants play as if they had a side bet with someone on who can last the longest. They very seldom bluff, and don't risk chips unless they have either a short stack or a big hand. My friend, the event normally lasts less than two hours. It is not that easy to get the nuts. A good satellite player is a good improviser, a person who hopes to beat the hand his opponent actually holds, instead of nearly all the hands his opponent might conceivably have. Good money poker players come in a variety of styles; good satellite poker players do not. You must be aggressive to win satellites.

Yes, aggression at the key moment is a necessity. However, that moment is in the later stages of play, and not in the early stages. Let's talk about this a bit.

The typical satellite format for hold'em is to have ten entrants. These players get three hundred dollars worth of chips apiece. The blinds start out at five and ten dollars, and go up— usually doubled—every fifteen or twenty minutes. So at the start, there are nine other players competing for a pot whose chips are only five percent of your full stack. How are you supposed to play in a many-handed game with a tiny pot? Tight, tighter, and tightest. Don't get into a big fight over nothing unless you are a strong favorite to win.

There is another element of satellite play that also dictates tight play at the start. Take a look at those other nine entrants.

There is another element of satellite play that also dictates tight play at the start. Take a look at those other nine entrants. What you rate to see at a typical table is three tough players, three average players, and three people that you have never seen before in your life. Of the three strangers, one will be so scared that you won't ever play a pot with him, and the other two will play like they are double-parked. With those two loosies, you are liable to get called if they have as much as king-high. They are not worried, because they "didn't expect to win anyway," want to see how you are playing, and can enter another satellite in a few minutes when they bust out in this one. The obvious correct strategy for the early stage of play is to do nothing fancy and simply wait for a good hand.

You will not be waiting long for the situation to change markedly. Often, half the field disappears by the time the blinds are raised for the first time, and the crazies figure to be gone. You are now playing in a five-handed game, and the blinds constitute ten percent of your stack instead of only five percent (unless you were lucky enough to snag a pot). It is time to play a little poker. Come out of that shell and get ready to gamble.

By this time you have had an opportunity to size up the other players. They are probably going to be gambling also. They don't figure to be holding a rock hand any more than you do. So if you get something reasonable like top pair, don't be making a big laydown.

One fact about hold'em that is of critical importance for the late stages of satellite play is that it is hard to get a large overlay before the flop. Pair over pair and suchlike is rare. The typical layout is more like A-Q vs K-9. Sure, the A-Q is favored, but not by as big a margin as many people think; it is less than a 2-to-1 favorite. There are plenty of spots in later stages of satellite play where you get caught trying to steal the blind money and now simply have to put the rest of your dough in and hope to draw out. There are also going to be a fair number of times where you reluctantly go with your hand hoping to improve and actually have the best hand already. So don't be gun-shy before the flop. A typical situation when the table has shrunk to three finalists is for the players to each have about a grand in chips, and the blinds to now be at least $50 and $100. Any time the blinds are ten percent of your stack and you are posting two out of three deals, you don't have much flexibility. A hand like Q-9 looks more than reasonable, and an ace is a monster. So be sure to readjust your hand value scale if you get to be a finalist.

As you can see, the most important quality of the skilled satellite player is the mental flexibility to adjust to the current situation at the table. In the space of less than an hour, you go from a rock to an aggressive player to a kamikaze pilot. The reward is nice. An average satellite player rates to win one out of ten satellite tournaments; a top player rates to win about two out of ten satellite tournaments. (If you don't believe this, I hope that you are around to bet me the next time I play in a series of pot-limit Omaha satellites.)

SHORTHANDED PLAY
by Bob Ciaffone

Do you play shorthanded poker? Before you say "No" answer these two questions: Do you ever play in poker tournaments? Do you ever find yourself one of the last four players in the pot, except for the blind or a forced bet? Obviously, you must answer "Yes" to at least the second question. Whatever our proclivities, we all need to know how to play shorthanded. To be sure, being one of the last four players in the pot is somewhat different from being one of four players dealt in at the beginning. The remaining deck stub figures to be richer in the desirable cards for that game, if a number of additional players have been dealt in and folded. The degree this affects the situation varies considerably with the form of poker being played. It is particularly noticeable at lowball draw and hold'em; at seven-card stud high or Omaha, it is a bit lesser in importance. But the other elements of shorthanded play other than a rich deck will apply.

If the game itself is shorthanded, the first question to ask yourself is, "Should I play in this game?" If it is the final stage of a poker tournament, you of course do not have a choice. But in a money game, you do not have to play.

The most important factor is who the other people are in the game. If they are inferior players, you may have a bigger overlay than in a full game. The type of player you wish to gamble with is the kind that plays only his own hand, without paying much attention to what you do. If you check, and he has nothing, he contentedly checks right along behind you. If you cannot beat this kind of weak player, we recommend taking up a game that has somewhat lesser emphasis on psychology, such as Scrabble or chess. You have no future in poker.

Inferior players come in all shapes and sizes. If your opponent knows poker well, but is overly aggressive and has no discipline, you have a better chance of parting him from his money in a full game. In fact, with the elements I have described, it may well be you who rates to be the loser in the setting I have portrayed.

Most of the time, a shorthanded game arises at either the beginning of a session, or at the end. Either way, there is a lot of social pressure to play, as one additional player can easily be the difference between having a game or not. In such situations, a smart gambler evaluates the situation objectively, rather than succumbing to peer pressure. Remember that everybody else's interest is actually diametrically opposed to yours. You want to increase your bankroll, whereas they want to diminish it. Most of the time, if you would be at a disadvantage, or have a limited amount of capital and feel your chances would be superior with a full table, the right thing to do is take a break or go home.

Do not fall into the trap of getting ego-involved, and feel you should not back off in any poker situation. I remember a no-limit hold-em game that occurred in the early eighties at the Horseshoe Casino during the World Series of Poker. I was in a fivehanded game with top pro players Ray Zee and Steve Lott, and a couple of weak players whose identity I have now forgotten. The two weakies got up and went to dinner, but left their chips on the table. The three of us wanted to hold the game together for their return, so we kept playing. I am a reasonable shorthanded no-limit hold-em player, although it is not my forte. And Ray Zee is likely one of the top dozen poker players in the world. But we both erred. Steve Lott is an absolutely murderous shorthanded player, and came pretty close to completely running over us. By the time the twosome returned from dinner, I had lost back all the money I had won earlier, and Zee also had a bad result. To add insult to injury, the two returning turkeys expressed dissatisfaction with the fact that no new players had taken a seat, and picked up their chips. (One may wonder who they thought was going to saunter in and kindly make up a fourth player for Steve, Ray, and me, without their own magnetic presence.) So the moral of the story is you are not under contract to play in any poker game.

Here is some of the ways shorthanded play differs from a full game, and the subsequent influence on strategy:

(1) Hand values are increased. A hand that rates to beat two other people does not need to be nearly as strong as one needed to beat seven other people. For example, top pair at hold'em

figures to be good enough to play for all your money, unless the chips are really deep. Top pair is even a reasonable Omaha hand, if there is nothing too terrifying on the board. So you need to get familiar with the hand values for the number of players arrayed against you.

(2) There are more moves. Giving a free card is not as dangerous, so a skilled shorthanded player is willing to check a good hand fairly often when he gets one. If you are up against aggressive players, this is necessary to stop them from running over you. Otherwise, it is too easy for them to adopt the policy of simply betting every time you check.

(3) Aggression becomes even more important. It is less likely that the opposition has a hand that can take pressure, so you bet and raise more often. The hold'em player that places a lot of emphasis on having outs before undertaking any aggressive action has standards too high for shorthanded play. Remember, the only prerequisite that is essential to bet is some chips in front of you.

(4) You must adjust every time a new player enters or leaves the game. For example, when you go from four players to five players, the number of players has increased by 25 percent. That is like going from eighthanded to tenhanded. So make the appropriate adjustment in hand values and tempo.

Here is the most important thing to know about being a strong shorthanded player. In big-bet poker, the fact that you have the leverage of betting a large amount in relation to the pot gives you a powerful cannon to fire. And as any good military commander or athletic coach will tell you, "If you've got a big gun, shoot it."

As you can see, knowing how to play shorthanded is an important part of anyone's poker education. It is foolish to avoid shorthanded play, as the value of playing in any poker game depends on the quality of the opponents, not their number. In a shorthanded game you get to participate far more often than in a full game. This gives you more opportunity to bring your skills to bear, and makes the game more fun as well.

32-POKER HISTORY
by Bob Ciaffone

Poker is thought to have originated in New Orleans shortly after 1800. It bears a resemblance to the English card game "Brag" and the Persian "As Nas," but nobody knows the exact circumstances or persons that created poker.

From New Orleans, poker spread rapidly throughout the Mississippi River Basin. The numerous riverboats were often a setting for high-stakes poker games, both honest and otherwise.

Poker in its original form was played with a stripped deck with only one betting round and no chance to improve the hand. By the middle of the nineteenth century the game had evolved into draw with a fifty-two card deck. The Civil War helped spread poker throughout the United States and it became our national card game.

In the latter part of the 19th century draw poker migrated to Europe via England. Even today, draw is the favored form of poker in a number of European countries such as Sweden and Italy. The scope of poker now includes the whole globe. For example, in 1992 I visited Nepal, a small country in the Himalayan mountains that has only been open to Westerners since 1950. At the home of one of the locals in their capital city Katmandu they had a weekly pot-limit Omaha eight-or-better game!

Limit betting is actually a modern invention. In the old days you could bet whatever money was in front of you whenever you wanted to; in other words, it was played no-limit table stakes. In most countries outside of North America, no-limit or pot-limit is the favored way to play the game. Many top European poker players never even played limit poker until they started visiting Las Vegas and other places in America.

In Hollywood movies, poker games are sometimes depicted with a rule that if you bet more than the opponent has in front of him, he must either scurry around town to raise the money or forfeit the pot. Such a rule would cause the wealthiest person playing in the game to have the power to win any pot by simply betting all his money. Why would anybody else play in such a game?

To the best of my knowledge this scenario is completely fictitious. I have browsed extensively through the special collections of old and rare books at the University of Nevada at Las Vegas university library, which has a lot of information on nineteenth century poker. In no place was there any reference to the stupid "comb the town" rule that motion pictures like to show. There is every indication poker has always used our present method of simply allowing players to call for what they have in front of them and refunding any extra amount wagered to the bettor.

Poker forms have evolved that are far removed from the draw games that were once the only method of play. Stud poker arrived around the time of the Civil War. Hold'em was invented in Texas during the early part of this century. World Champion Johnny Moss says he played the game in Dallas when it was introduced there in 1925. A number of old-time Texas players told me they thought the game originated in Robb's Town, Texas (near Corpus Christi) around the time of the First World War, and this is probably as good as guess as any. Omaha reached Las Vegas in 1982, and London in 1984. There are many poker forms played in other countries that are unknown in the United States. Some examples are "Irish" in England, "Sowsum" in Canada, and "Manila" in Southeast Asia.

The most prominent example of the use of big-bet poker is the annual event determining the World Champion for that year. This is the four-day $10,000 buy-in no-limit hold'em contest held every spring at Binion's Horseshoe Casino in Las Vegas. Both Stewart and I favor the pot-limit and no-limit cash games, but tournament events using this type of betting are very popular. Most tournaments have a final gala event to crown a champion, and the poker form for this is normally no-limit hold'em. Perhaps some of you readers will eventually put the knowledge of big-bet poker gained from us to good use by going out and winning a major poker championship.

33-BUSINESS
by Stewart Reuben

It is common practice in big-bet poker for business to be done when all the money has been wagered and there are still cards to come. This is often called a settlement in Las Vegas. It may be common but it isn't to be encouraged; it slows down the game and confuses outsiders, or makes them think the game is being carved up.

Legitimate examples. In Omaha the flop is J-10-4. One player has A-K-Q-9 and the other J-J-5-5. This is so close to even money it makes no difference. The players may decide to split the pot. I once had a made straight on sixth street in seven-card stud against Frank Thompson with trips and four to a flush. All the money was in and we had seen many cards, several of them useful to him. We agreed I should take £5000 out of the pot and he £4000, then we would play for the rest. This took about five seconds. This wasn't permitted practice at the Victoria Casino but the manager said, "They're good friends. Nobody else was ever involved and this is the biggest pot of the year. We'll let it go." Common-sense on his part. Once two players have reached an agreement, it is usually too late to do anything about it. They will simply settle up outside the building once they are told it is illegal. At least this way, everybody knows what is going on. Incidentally, Frank was asked, rather naively, "You're good friends with Stewart. How come you played such a large pot?" He answered, just as I would have, "It wouldn't be much of a friendship if mere money came in the way."

Tables have been drawn up, especially for hold'em and Omaha (the latter often incorrectly) to show the precise odds of two hands against each other. The underdog may win 40% of the time. Thus the favorite takes insurance against this happening, possibly with a third party. He bets on his opponent, receiving 4-3 odds instead of the correct 3-2. You notice, the third party has done very nicely, thank you. He has picked up a winning percentage play without even being in the game.

You are only supposed to be playing if you can afford a loss. Thus the only reason for taking insurance or doing business is if you have the best of it. Other than that, what is the point of shoveling all your money into a pot and then removing much of it after all the action has taken place?

Another important point is that doing business wastes time. As with other commercial activities, time means money in poker—especially if you are paying a table charge. Even if not, life is too short to wait around for two players to decide who has the edge and by how much. In fact, insurance caused pot-limit high-low split Omaha to vanish, so much time and energy was spent on the discussions.

One legitimate way to spread the risk, especially in flop games such as hold'em or Omaha, is to deal out the pot twice. e.g. all the money is in with one card to come. Then a card is burnt and a card dealt faceup for one-half the pot. This is repeated for the second half. Precise splitting doesn't have to be done if both players are agreeable. This helps reduce the slings and arrows of outrageous fortune and requires no discussion. You do not even have to see your opponent's holding before coming to this arrangement. It can even be done in multihanded action pots.

Some strong players believe no such concessions should ever be made. The weaker player will be more relaxed as they have a chance of saving something from the wreckage. Others consider it desirable to make the weaker player feel at home. I have an ambivalent attitude but tend towards the latter. However I almost never initiate such discussions.

34-POT-LIMIT RULES
By Bob Ciaffone

Pot-limit rules differ somewhat from limit poker. Having full knowledge of the rules can make a difference in your results. Here are the rules of pot-limit play, as used in most public cardrooms. The first four rules also apply to no-limit play.

(1) There is no limitation on the number of raises. The reason is at big-bet poker the pot size grows so quickly no restriction is necessary. (I have never seen more than a bet and four raises on any pot-limit deal, and I have seen four raises only once.)

(2) The amount raised must at least equal the amount of the previous bet or raise, unless a player is going all-in. (If Player A bets $100 and Player B raises $200, Player C wishing to reraise must wager at least $200 more. The total bet to Player C was $300, but the minimum amount he could reraise was only $200, the amount of the previous raise.)

Some cardrooms require that a raise in this situation be $300, thus doubling the total bet. This may actually be the better rule for multihanded pots, as it protects the player from being whipsawed with a series of small raises.

A few places allow short raises in heads-up play. I feel strongly there should be no exceptions. We must avoid any misunderstandings, and protect inexperienced players from facing peculiar situations that have no counterpart at limit play. It is unfair to let a player who announces "raise" to simply throw one more chip into the pot if it looks like he's getting called, and sometimes simply saying "raise" causes the opponent to fold without finding out how much the raise is.

(3) A short bet or raise—possible when someone goes all-in—does not reopen the betting. (This contrasts with limit poker, where a bet or raise need only be half a full bet to reopen the betting.) Example: Player A bets $100, Player B raises all-in for $80 more (the total bet is now $180), and Player C calls the $180. At big-bet poker, Player A may not reraise.

(4) A player is entitled to know approximately how much money an adversary is playing. For this reason, it is a good idea to require that all cash be converted into chips, which are easier to eyeball and count. Unfortunately, these days outside factors such as government regulation of large cash transactions may prevent this ideal from being achieved. Even so, any bill other than the largest denomination in regular circulation—$100's for Americans—should not be permitted.

In most situations, it suffices for the opponent to simply move his arms out of the way so you can get an approximation of his money. In exceptional circumstances involving a multihanded pot where you need to know if an all-in wager will be reopening the betting, an opponent may be asked to furnish an exact count.

Chips of an unusually high value should not be permitted. For example, I have seen costly mistakes in a $1,000 buy-in game when someone had a $5,000 chip among his holdings. Higher-denomination chips that are allowed should be kept where they are visible to opponents, and not concealed behind other chips to bushwhack an unaware adversary.

(5) The pot size may be rounded off, to make the maximum allowable bet a convenient number according to the denomination of chips used in the game. An odd amount rounds off upward to the nearest smooth number. For example, suppose the blinds are $5, $10, and $25, and the minimum bring-in is $25. Player A calls, the middle blind calls, and the big blind wishes to raise the maximum amount. The pot size is now $80 ($25 from Player A's call, $5 from the small blind, $25 from the middle blind's call, and $25 from Player B's call prior to raising). If the rules of the game call for all bets to be in $25 increments, Player B may raise $100, even though the pot actually contains only $80. The odd $5 is counted as $25. (Some places prefer to use a rounding off rule that says the odd amount must be more than half a bet to be rounded upwards.)

(6) No one may overbet the pot, even in heads-up situations. The reasoning is simple. If the cardroom's floor personnel tell a prospective player the game is pot-limit, he is entitled to play

without having to face a bet greater than the pot size. Therefore, the dealers should be instructed to call attention to an overbet and trim the amount down to proper size in **all** situations. Some people say the overbet can only work in favor of the person bet into, because that person has the option of calling the whole thing or requiring the bet to be trimmed down. They would leave it up to the target to call down an overbet. This reasoning is incorrect. First, the player may not realize an overbet has occurred. Second, asking the bet be trimmed down looks weak, conveying information about your hand to which the opponent is not entitled. (Stewart has been known to require an opponent's bet be trimmed down to legal size in observance of the rules, and then raise the bettor.)

(7) If the dealer and other players fail to call attention to an overbet, and the opponent calls, the bet stands. The reason is to prevent a player who violated the rules by overbetting the pot from profiting thereby. For example, suppose the pot is $300, and Player A bets $500 at Player B. Nobody says anything. Player B thinks it over and calls the full amount. Player A should not be permitted to retrieve $200 from the pot by now calling attention to his own overbet. Obviously, it is unfair to let Player A confront his opponent with what looks like a large bet, and then take money out of the pot if the full amount gets called. This can be a difficult situation for the decision-maker, because Player B is not supposed to speedily call the full amount before the dealer has had any opportunity to call attention to the overbet. It is up to the decision-maker to determine who is trying to shoot an angle. In a close situation, I would rule in favor of Player B, because his opponent was the one who clearly broke the rules.

There should be a point where a wager has been acted on—condoned—by sufficient number of players that it should stand, even though there is someone who has not yet acted. When something improper happens in a game there is an obligation to speak up about it as soon as possible, and not gain information by delaying the complaint. The rule in Stewart's game is when two players have acted on a wager its size is accepted by all.

35-DEALING BIG-BET POKER
by Bob Ciaffone

Even non-dealers should be familiar with the proper rules and procedure for dealing big-bet poker. This enables the player to protect his rights and encourage the proper running of the game.

It is more difficult to deal pot-limit poker than limit poker. There is the additional mental burden of keeping track of the pot size, and policing overbets. Pot-limit players are usually quite experienced, have a good knowledge of how the game should be run, and tend to be fussier about it than limit players. Also, dealer errors tend to be more costly at pot-limit. On the other hand, a good dealer is certainly appreciated by the players, and hopefully given the appropriate monetary reward (via tokes) for being competent.

The initial requirement for dealing pot-limit is a thorough knowledge of rules and procedures used in the game. See our preceding chapter "Pot-limit Poker Rules" on this.

Here are some tips on being a good pot-limit dealer:

(1) Always keep track of the pot size by mental arithmetic. Do not rely on stacking the chips for a count. In fact, most players feel that stacking the chips is not just unnecessary, but unwanted. It draws too much attention to the pot size. (A good dealer will learn to use some easy mental shortcuts to aid in computing quickly. For example, if one player bets the size of the pot and the next player wants to raise the maximum, the total amount needed by the raiser is four times the pot size.)

(2) Do not announce the pot size unless specifically asked by a player. The announcement "I'm going to raise" should be treated simply as a player protecting himself against a charge of string-betting, and not an inquiry as to the maximum allowable bet. Pot-limit play differs from most limit games by allowing the bettor to choose how much to bet. The alert player attaches a lot of importance to the amount an opponent bets. In a game that requires the dealer to announce the pot size every time a player is about to bet or raise, many more wagers are the full size of the pot. Furthermore, special attention is indirectly drawn to any

wager that is not the limit. A rule that lets the dealer's mouth strongly influence the betting, and prevents the natural flow of information conveyed by the bet size, is certainly a bad rule.

(3) If you think a player may be overbetting the pot size, announce how much is in the pot, and trim down any excess. Example: If there is $500 in the pot, and a player moves in a stack of chips that may exceed that amount, say "$500 is all you can bet." If you don't know the pot size (presumably because the action is moving very fast) simply say "he bets the pot" when someone makes an obvious overbet. You have then protected both the player and his opponent, and can comfortably straighten out the exact amount.

(4) Even though there is a rule that says the placing of a single chip or bill in the pot is only a call unless the player has said "raise," the dealer should make the appropriate statement of "call" or "raise" whenever this happens. An oral announcement makes matters crystal clear. He should also change the chip or bill immediately if the player only called. These actions by the dealer are very helpful in preventing any misunderstandings.

(5) When a pot with equalized original bets is getting raised, it is usually better for the dealer to take those original bets into the center pot. (This occurs, for example, when the big blind wishes to raise.) Taking in the original bets lets the dealer have better control over the subsequent action.

(6) In a threeway pot with one player all-in, do not take in the extra chips bet on the side and put them together for a sidepot. Leave them in front of the players who bet them, and simply announce that they constitute the sidepot. That way, it is easier for everyone to remember at the showdown which players are involved in the sidepot. You should ask for the sidepot hands to be shown first. This avoids the unfortunate situation where a player involved only in the main pot shows down a big hand, and a sidepot contender unthinkingly throws his hand away.

(7) In a pot where a large number of players get all-in, it may be a time-saving idea to leave each player's individual bet in front of him. Hopefully, the person with the most money will show up with the best hand, saving several minutes of bookwork.

(8) It is part of the dealer's responsibility to help players get information to which they are entitled. Don't allow concealed hands, hidden high-denomination chips, and that sort of thing. On the other hand, don't be a motormouth that announces each player's action with a running commentary. Good judgment by the dealer about when to speak and what to say is helpful.

(9) Always remember that pot-limit players have many decisions that are not easy, and are far-reaching in their financial consequences. Do not try to force the pace of play as if the game were a crew of rookies in a low-stakes game. Such dealer methods as pointing to each player as the action proceeds around the table, or saying "It's on you" to a player that pauses to think, have no place in a pot-limit game. To be sure, the dealer should wake up a player who does not know it is his turn to act. Beyond that, it is better to let the game flow at a natural pace.

Dealers are taught how to deal only limit poker; pot-limit dealing procedure is usually neglected. A good pot-limit dealer is hard to find, and players should show their appreciation generously when they are lucky enough to get one.

36-THE HOUSE CHARGE
by Stewart Reuben

The house percentage is also known as the rake, vigorish, table charge, or cut. Wherever you play poker, except privately (and often even then), you have to pay for the privilege. This fee is usually taken as a percentage of the pot or a certain sum per hour.

I have often heard it said that the amount you pay doesn't matter; it is the losers who pay on behalf of the winners. In a sense this is true, but I am certain I have paid about $150,000 in table charges since taking up the game. Also, sad to relate, I am sometimes a loser. Anyway, other people say it is the *winners* who pay. This is certainly true if the losers have financial limits.

Many games charge 5% of the pot, and you are expected to tip the dealers about 1% on top. This is very heavy and hard to overcome in a big-bet game. Since most pots are two-handed, effectively it is a 10% tax. e. g. you put $100 into the pot and so does your opponent. You receive back $190, a $90 win for a $100 investment.

In earlier days in Las Vegas, pots at limit poker were raked as much as the dealer could get away with. There is the story that at one casino there was just a drunk playing and all the others at the table were shills or proposition players. This did not stop the drunk running all over the game. Finally, he won yet another hand and the dealer scooped up not only the entire pot, but also some of the drunk's own money. It was not easy to win in a game like that.

Nowadays, a much lower percentage is taken from smaller games, and this is capped at about $3. In the larger games, there is a table charge. Those I play in at Las Vegas currently charge $10 per hour, which is relatively tiny.

It is illegal to cut the pot in England, and also forbidden to toke the dealer. The latter is unfortunate, as it gives dealers little incentive to be efficient. I have played in games where the hourly rate is as high as £25 ($40 at the current rate of exchange). The huge game described in the London lowball chapter even had an exorbitant table charge of £50 per hour in its early days.

If my seat must find £25 every hour and I am a winner, then the losers at the table must pay not only their time, but also split mine amongst them.

When you play in a game which is raked rather than there being a table charge, you must adjust your style. It is essential to play tighter. Otherwise, the rake is going to get you, just like the bogey-man you feared as a child. If the total table charge by whatever system is too high, then it is possible for all the players to end up losers—especially if there is only a limited number in the school.

Now you can understand the term GHM, going home money. In games with high rakes this is your reward at the end of a long session—the house furnishing your cab fare home.

37-ETHICS AND COURTESY
by Bob Ciaffone

As a big-bet poker player, a higher standard of behavior is expected of you than in most low-stakes limit poker games. We felt obliged to include this section in our book to point out those poker standards that should be applied to a game played by ladies and gentleman. Here is a list of poker etiquette.

(1) At big-bet poker, the amount of money in front of an opponent has a very strong effect on how we play a hand. A player is entitled to accurate information in this respect. He may ask, "How deep are you?," and the recipient of this query usually states an approximate figure. Sometimes the queried person will lift his arms and let the opponent get a view of his chips, which is usually sufficient. It is improper to conceal large denomination chips behind smaller denomination chips, or any such action that would deliberately mislead an opponent as to the amount of money in front of you. It is also improper to use chips to conceal your hand so that players on your left are unaware of your presence in the pot.

(2) Collusion between players in a game is of course prohibited. Players should avoid even the appearance of impropriety. Out of order are soft-play agreements, potting out, agreeing to save a sum of money before the flop, or any other action that builds an "us and them" attitude. Particularly bad is agreeing not to bet the opponent when a third person is all-in. Frankly, this is a form of cheating. You are really saying, "Let's give ourselves a better chance to win the pot at the expense of this other guy."

(3) It is considered impolite to ask to see an opponent's hand that one has just beaten in a pot. Besides being rude, in most cases you are giving the opponent another chance to find something he overlooked. Even if you are not the pot-winner, you should be careful that your query does not give a player a second shot at the pot. I remember a pot-limit Omaha game as Caesar's Palace in Las Vegas that took place during a "Super Bowl of Poker" tournament. I flopped the under-full in a three-way pot

that eventually totaled about $8,000. At the showdown one of my opponents tabled a full house. As the other one started to throw his hand away, I asked him, "What were your kickers?" I was curious how much duplication there was between my opponent's hands, as they had obviously both flopped trips and were trying to fill. The person to whom I made this stupid inquiry stopped in the middle of his discarding swing and showed his hand. It was discovered that one of his kickers matched a boardcard and made him a bigger full house. The poor fellow who lost the eight grand because of my mouth reminds me of this incident whenever I run into him at a poker tournament. It is not one of my fond memories. Please don't ask to see a hand until it has been released into the muck. I still feel badly about the pain my inquiry caused.

(4) A player should always make his actions crystal clear. If you put a big chip into the pot for a call, say "call." Even though there is a rule that if you do not say "raise" it is a call, don't leave anyone wondering about your intention. Learn to cut chips into the pot so your bet is neatly stacked and easy to read properly. If you are pausing to decide what to do, say "time" and make sure the players behind you do not act out-of-turn.

(5) Smoking will not boost your popularity. A good player is always interested in getting an invitation to a new game. While there is such a thing as a "polite smoker," he still is not as welcome as a polite nonsmoker.

(6) Most players do not like a short-handed game. A player who is frequently absent from the table hurts a game and will create some resentment. Also unpopular is a motor-mouth. Some talking is of course okay, but yakking loudly while some poor fellow facing a big bet is trying to decide what to do is certainly poor form. Do your conversing between hands. Doubly bad is endlessly discussing how a hand was played or should have been played. Out-of-place is any activity that interferes with your obligation to act promptly on your hand, such as heated discussions or newspaper reading. Please pay attention to the game. We are trying to mold you into a winning player. Any of the above-mentioned activities are improper poker behavior,

will make others resent your presence, and thus will cost you money. Show some class; win cleanly and graciously.

(7) The responsibility for your result—including a bad one—is your own. The dealer is not the cause. Either you played badly, or you were unlucky. It is disgusting to see a player make a serious error and start chastising the dealer after the hand. And on occasion an opponent does something so dumb you could not have anticipated such a play, but this causes you to make a misjudgment. Please say absolutely nothing, and simply make a mental note for future situations.

38-CHEATING
by Bob Ciaffone

It is an unfortunate attribute of human nature that money brings out the darker side in some people. Big-bet poker is usually played for sizable sums, which can attract the attention of unscrupulous persons. A player of this kind of poker needs to know how to protect himself against the bad element that may become an unwelcome presence.

Who may be a cheater? Almost anybody. Here is a letter that was printed in advice columnist Abby Van Buren's column back in 1977:

Dear Abby: What do you think of a grown man who cheats at cards, and when confronted, throws the cards up in the air, runs to his room and broods for the rest of the evening? Abby, this man has a Ph.D. in nuclear physics and holds a high paying job.

Even though a cheater is more likely to be some type of lowlife character, nobody should be totally exempted from suspicion simply because of holding a high social position.

While the chance of being cheated on a given occasion is quite slim, the odds are heavily in favor of encountering this problem at some point in your poker career. As is said at the start of a boxing match, "Protect yourself at all times."

There are four basic kinds of cheating. The first is cheating by the dealer in collusion with a player, the second is cheating by the dealer acting alone, the third is cheating between players, and the fourth is by a player acting alone. The most dangerous kind is that done by the dealer, although collusion between players is the most common form.

Let's talk first about cheating by the dealer. We are referring to a public cardroom or other game site where the dealer is there to deal the cards and does not play in the game himself. This type of cheating is rare because the dealer usually would not want to take the chance of losing his job and getting barred from the industry, but it still occurs once in a while.

If you do encounter a cheating dealer, he or she is likely to be very good at it. Don't expect to be able to see the cheating itself. An adept dealer can use a false shuffle and deal seconds—dealing the second card instead of the top card—without detection by the naked eye, even a trained one.

Your first line of defense against a cheating dealer is having good procedures by the house to prevent this sort of thing. For example, the most damaging form of cheating is the "cold deck," a deck that is stacked ahead of time and then run into the game. To stop this, the house procedure should be that any new deck must be fanned out faceup on the table for inspection and then turned facedown and thoroughly scrambled before being used. If the deck has been previously in use and is being switched back in, it still must be scrambled before using.

Of course, the deck must be cut before dealing. This should be done with one hand only, using a clean release by the other hand. The dealer should never be allowed to leave the deck half-cut in two piles on the table while the dealer performs some other operation such as taking in antes. This would allow a player to locate a card, and there is some danger of the two halves being put back together in the same order they came apart, nullifying the cut.

The dealer cannot give a confederate a made-up hand unless he knows where the cards are. Therefore, at the end of every deal, the player's discards should be intermingled with the remaining stock of the deck in a random manner. If the dealer puts discards on top of the unused cards in a manner that a card can be located, this is at the very least a faulty procedure. If you see the dealer picking up discards in a deliberate manner and putting them on top of the new deck being made up, fold the next hand and see which player winds up with those cards.

To use a crooked deal, the dealer must select the cards he wants to give his confederates and put them on top of the deck before he starts his shuffle. Once he starts shuffling, you won't be able to detect anything improper, so the time to catch on to a cheater is the way he assembles discarded cards.

This is a good time to point out that cards should be faced away from the dealer when he picks up discards and squares up the deck at the end of a deal. Many British poker dealers, in an effort to make sure the players do not see and locate any cards, face the deck toward themselves. This is bad. Frankly, the dealer is in far better position to damage you if he knows where the cards are than any player would be. Once again, the house should require procedures that protect the player in the best way.

Occasionally someone, either the dealer or a player, will try to palm a chip and remove it from the pot. Playing poker where there is a surveillance camera helps deter this type of thievery. We recommend the use of a "betting line," an oval line that demarks the pot area. This line must be crossed by chips going into the pot for it to be a legal bet. This line encourages the players to put their bets where the dealer can easily reach them—and makes it more difficult for the player to retrieve any chips from the pot.

I am only aware of one dealer who stole chips from the pot on a regular basis. {Lucky Bob; I've known more. SR} He was a heavy sports bettor, and apparently not too successful at it. The man was finally caught and barred from the industry. I suppose the house could refuse to hire dealers with a sports-betting habit, but undoubtedly this would cut down too much on the available labor pool. Actually, it is hard to catch this type of thief, so we are fortunate that he is so rare.

In most home games, and sometimes even in a casino, the players themselves deal the cards. Cheating is much more prevalent in this type of situation. The American method is to have a player shuffle the cards, get the deck cut by the player on his right, and then proceed to deal. This inferior system of letting the same player shuffle that is going to deal asks for trouble. Much better is the English method of having the player to the left of the dealer shuffle and the player on the dealer's right cut the cards.

One of the more dangerous types of cheaters is the holdout artist. This fellow is adept at palming a card, moving it to a storage place such as the kneepit, and switching it back into the game to make a winning hand at the opportune moment. Do not expect to see anything funny if the player is adept at this maneuver. And only in the movies would you ever find a mechanical holdout machine being used. A cheat wants to be in a position to deny accusations, so he is not going to endanger himself by using a contraption whose discovery would leave no room for doubt about his guilt. Rather, the way to defeat him is for the house to have the dealer regularly count the deck stub at the end of the deal. You won't know who is doing the cheating for sure, but at least you'll know if any monkey business is going on.

Perhaps the best-known cheating method is marking the cards. A type of daub can be used for this which is only visible through special contact lenses. (You don't even need glasses these days.) The only way this can be detected is to have the deck of cards tested at a laboratory.

Fortunately, this type of cheating is not as deadly as one might assume. The cheater does not know what cards will be coming, because the dealer burns the top card first. You should hold your cards in a manner that only a corner of them is peeking out. (It is unethical to completely conceal your hand.) Far more common than daub-marked cards are nail-marked cards. Nail marks may either be purposeful or unintentional. And often a manufacturers defect such as a small white circular area will be visible on the cards. For these reasons the same deck of cards should not be used for an excessive length of time in the game.

The most common type of cheating is when two players in the game are partners. One of them signals when he has a good hand, and then slowplays it. The other one puts in a modest-size raise and sends the whole field into the jaws of death. For this type of cheating—which is much more effective in pot-limit than limit play—it is easy to become suspicious and hard to prove anything. It certainly helps a lot to know your players. Make a mental note when this type of play happens in the game and see if it is frequently the same two particular players involved.

You all too often see a couple of players who refuse to bet each other when they are heads-up in a pot. Likely they are **not** cheating. Cheaters would be making an effort to disguise what they are doing. Rather, the players are pals who have a misguided idea of how friends should act when they play in the same game. I suggest the "soft-players" be informed that they must either change their ways or not play in the same game at the same time. Such behavior builds an us-and-them feeling that creates a bad gambling atmosphere.

When you think you've discovered cheating of any kind, here is how to act. Do not get confrontational. The cheater of course denies everything, and will try to make you out a quick-triggered paranoid that is the real culprit in the act. You might even get in a fight. If you are so tough this thought does not dismay you, keep in mind that there are such things as knives and guns. A cheater may well be armed in anticipation of trouble.

The right way to act is to simply quit the game. Warn your friends in private about what you've seen. Frankly, there are some players (myself included, though it was in the distant past) who have on occasion decided to play in a game even after finding out there is some cheating going on. Sometimes the game is so good and the other players —including the cheaters—so bad that you would be hurting your pocketbook too much to quit. I, of course, hesitate to recommend continuing in such a situation to you, but quitting is not the only option.

To sum up, remember to play in places that have good procedures to protect you against thieves. The house having proper anti-cheating procedures is your most important defense against a thief. And do not flex your muscles or start wagging your finger when you run into cheating. Be discreet. Don't get beaten up, sued for slander, or create a lifelong enemy.

39-PROBABILITY CONCEPTS
"Don't Believe Everything You Have Read"

by Stewart Reuben

I am not referring here to the simple probability of your making a hand, but about the odds of your winning and losing money in a given hand. Remember that we keep score in poker by counting our money at the end of the session, not by the number of winning hands we make.

IMPLIED ODDS

The pot is $100 and you face a bet of $100. Thus the pot now stands at $200, and you are receiving 2-1 for your money. It is sixth street in seven-card stud, or there is one card to come in Omaha. In both cases it will be about 4-1 against your making a flush. Thus you shouldn't call heads-up. But several books suggest that, if there are players yet to come, then you can include the implication that they will call if you do. Thus, if you think two are going to call, now you have 4-1 for your money. **This is absolute nonsense.** Each of these players may pass, they may call, or they may raise. You do not know what is in their minds.

Correctly, the term "implied odds" refers to the amount of money extra to that already in the pot you are likely to win if you make your draw. Here is a good example from Omaha. Your hand is A♥-10♠-2♥-2♠. The board is K♥-Q♠-7♥-2♦. In other words, you have hit the mystery trips on fourth street. The pot is $1000, you are last to speak, and the only other player bets $1000, having led out on the flop. You will win with eight hearts, one deuce, and certainly not lose the pot with a jack. Thus you have 12 outs. But you can only see eight cards, and are assuming the opposition has three kings. Thus you win only with 12 cards in 42. This is worse than 2 to 1; in fact 2.5 to 1. If a flush comes, you cannot expect to be paid off. If a jack comes, you may split the pot.

If not, there is a very fair chance he will come out betting, or check and call your bet, thinking you are bluffing. If the fourth deuce comes, not only is he going to come out betting, but he is going to stand a raise and may even reraise. Passing this hand would be madness. Strangely enough, from your viewpoint, it is better if he has trips rather than two pair, if you intend to pass a bet at the river if the board blanks. This is because you have a much better chance of being paid off if you hit the nuts. By the way, if the board blanks or pairs and he checks, do not assume your trips are winning and automatically bet. He may be lurking in the grass.

This concept of implied odds is a sufficiently important poker concept for us to take another example. In hold'em you have 10♥-8♥. The board is 9♥-6♣-2♥-K♠. You have three nut outs and a further nine hearts which may also be winning. Facing a near pot-size bet, you must assess the likelihood of your being called if you make the hand. Certainly the odds are inadequate on their own.

It is always an advantage to act last in such cases. You are far more likely to be called if you are last to speak rather than if you must come out betting. In addition, what are you going to do if a heart arrives at the river and he bets out? Your flush is not the biggest.

Sometimes you must play intelligently after all the cards have been dealt in order to receive the implied odds you imagined existed. e.g. at Omaha, you hold A♥-Q♥-Q-10 and the flop comes J♥-6♥-2♣. John is to speak before you, and Ann after. The pot stands at $100. John checks; you bet $100 with an overpair and the nut flush-draw. Ann calls, as does John. The board now brings (J♥-6♥-2♣) 8♠. The pot is $400. John checks, you bet $300, and Ann raises $1000. John calls. What is going on, and do you have value for a call? John's holding is a mystery, but Ann presumably has trips. You must pay $1000 to win $3300. It is most unlikely neither has any of your cards, and certainly a queen may not win you the pot. In fact, it may prove to be a trouble card. They will probably both pass if a non-pairing flush card arrives. However, you may do very nicely if a 9 comes up.

The last card is the (J♥-6♥-2♣-8♠) 9♦, making you the nut straight. Now John bets $2000. This small amount is disappointing. The correct play is just to call. Now Ann may call without any straight, because she can gain $8300 out there for just $2000. The fact we know trips is worthless is irrelevant. If you were to raise, John, an intelligent player who may be bluffing, will only call if he is sharing the pot—or possibly if he has the under-straight. You must normally be content with $2000. Time and again I have seen players raise in this situation. What they hope to gain out of it, I cannot imagine. By the way, similarly if you are in John's position, it is better to come out betting than to trap. If the next player is doing his job and has the same straight, he will just smooth-call and hope to gain money from losing callers. If you check and the second player bets, the sandwiched player may be more likely to pass, fearing the possibility of a raise from you.

I was rather dismissive of making assumptions about how players yet to act will behave. Sometimes a reasonable assessment can be made, as in the following hand I played in Las Vegas in February, 1994. At pot limit Omaha the first player to speak bet, the second raised the pot, and I called with 9♥-8♠-7♥-5♣. Three more players called. The first player now raised the pot all-in for $2000. The second player called for $500. I had bundles left but none of the three following players had more than $2000; in fact two had less. I correctly assumed the first player had aces. Whether I had adequate odds is unknown to me. But I surmised, once I called, they would follow suit, rather like lemmings. I had my implied odds. Thus I called, the others went all-in, and I won the pot. I wonder if the hand would have been so memorable had another player scooped the pool?

ODDS WITH SEVERAL CARDS TO COME

Again, this is badly misunderstood in pot-limit or no-limit. You hold (A♥ K♥) 2♥ 9♥ in seven card stud. There are no other hearts on board. It is checked to you. You bet, and Harry (a vigorous player whom you know stylistically has at least two pair and is locked in to the bitter end) raises the pot-size of $100. It is now going to cost you $100 to win $200. We know it is about even money to make a flush in the next three cards. But are your money odds truly 2-1? If you call, the pot is now $300. You haven't made the flush and he bets out $300. You call. The pot is $900. If you decide to call on sixth street, despite not improving, you will have wagered $1300 to win $1400. This is not quite the 2-1 you had in mind. If you raise on fourth street and the two of you get all-in, then you will be receiving only slightly better than even money, as already shown.

Here is a paradox. Had you taken him all-in on fourth street, then your odds were reasonable. If you call on fourth street, setting your mind to call on fifth and sixth, unless he breaks out into an open pair; **then** on sixth street it is a mistake to call. You are a 4-1 underdog. Yet, you have avoided the full house disaster until seventh street. Why was going all-in okay and playing along all wrong?

If you have an extremely live four-flush and he has two pair, what are the true odds against winning the pot from fourth street? Although two pair have only four improving cards and are thus nearly 10-1 on each card, overall they are only about 3-1 against filling up. Thus they hit 25% of the time. You can only win 75% of the hands, and this reduces your winning hands to 40%, a 3-2 dog. Let us hope this explodes the myth that you should pour your money in on fourth street with a four-flush. Once you fear two pair, or the dreaded trips, you should switch off.

Four cards to an up-and-down straight has eight outs rather than the nine of a flush and, what's more, is a lower-ranking hand. However, it has one great advantage over a flush-draw. If you make it on fifth or sixth street, you are much more likely to be called. Your implied odds are enormous.

In both hold-em and Omaha, you are approximately a 7-4 dog to make a flush with two cards to come. With a board such as 8♥-4♣-2♥ and you holding A♥-J♥, you may well also win with an ace or jack. In Omaha, if you hold A♥-A♣-Q♦-7♥, you should fear that an ace will give you a loser. If the heart pairs the board, you will be traumatized by the fear of a full house, which is why we recommend only thinking in terms of nut outs in that game.

REVERSE IMPLIED ODDS

The "reverse implied odds" is the amount of money lost that results from completing a draw, yet failing to win the pot because the opponent either has or makes a better hand. Here is an example. A grand is in the pot. You hold (K♠ 2♠) 9♠ 2♥ J♠ 4♣ at seven stud. Your opponent has (? ?) A 9 3 7. He check-raised you on fifth street and bets $1000 on sixth street. You have seen only two other cards, the 2♦ and 2♣. Should you call?

Clearly you have only 9 outs from 40 cards, and thus the bare odds are inadequate. The implied odds must be considered. Let us assume he will check on the river, irrespective of his holding. Provided he has at least aces up, the typical player will call your river bet. Thus you determine not to bluff at all. If you call, 31 hands out of 40 you lose $1000 (-$31,000). On the other nine hands, you make the flush and bet $3000 (+$45,000). This seems quite a juicy price. But he has 4 chances in 40 of making a full house. In that case, which arises statistically on one of the hands where you make the flush, he check-raises you and you pass circumspectly. Thus you hit the flush eight hands, winning $5000 on each (+$40,000). One hand you lose an extra $3000 (-4,000). Thus your implied win for this hand is not $45,000, but $36,000. This is because of the reversal that can occur. Your profit over 40 hands is $5000, for an outlay of $40,000. This is a very healthy 12.5% and certainly cannot be passed up. Of course, in real life he doesn't invariably call. But on the other hand, you don't invariably pass his check-raise.

This type of reasoning is hardly ever relevant in limit poker. You invariably have adequate odds for your money for such a draw. In no-limit, with the added potential of being able to bet more than the pot, the implied odds really blossom.

In Omaha, the "reverse implied odds" are a major consideration when you have called a couple of players to make a straight with two cards to come and there is a two-flush on the board. You may well make your straight and yet be beaten either by a full or flush. In lowball draw, you must consider the reversal very seriously. You cannot pass all your drawing hands, and if you await a draw to the stone-cold nuts, the antes will swallow you up. In London lowball, you must never call a pot bet in order to make a hand such an 8 low, where the opponent may be holding an apparent 9 or 10 low, but is drawing under you to make a 7. Only in hold'em is the reversal of relatively less importance, because so many pots there are won by less than the maximum possible hand.

THE TILT FACTOR

There is another factor at work when we take a wide view of the term "implied odds." Certain steamers figure to go on tilt if they lose a big pot. Hitting a longshot against them like a middle-pin straight may send them over the moon. Here is a hand where the tilt factor was taken into account.

At Omaha, Stewart Q-Q-9-8. Flop Q-3-3. Chris Bjorin led out, Stewart called, and Jimmy raised. Chris passed and Stewart called. On fourth street, Stewart checked, Jimmy bet, and Stewart called. At the river Stewart checked and Jimmy bet. There was 30K in the pot. Stewart had discounted Chris's bet as a herring, and knew Jimmy might have 3-3. Anyway, he raised the remaining 5K and Jimmy called, showing down the quads. Stewart's sole reason for raising was that Jimmy would have gone on tilt in a big way had he lost the pot, perhaps blowing another 50K. Divided among the other five players at the table, that comes to 10K for Stewart. Thus he had 3-1 for his extra 5K, not mere even money.

40-FIGURING THE ODDS
by Bob Ciaffone

A limit poker player can get by with knowing only the approximate odds on a few simple situations. At big-bet poker, a good player needs to know precise information about the odds on a wide range of situations, and how those odds are computed.

Computing the odds on making a hand with one card to come is quite easy. There are 52 cards in a standard poker deck. Some will be known to you, and most will be unknown. You simply figure the number of unknown cards that make your hand and divide it into the number of unknown cards that leave you a loser. This ratio will be the odds on making the hand.

Here is an example. On fourth street in a hold'em game the board is K♥-9♥-6♠-4♣. Your hand is A♥-3♥, giving you the nut flush-draw. Suppose you need to hit the flush to win the pot. What are your chances?

In this problem six cards are known to you, leaving 46 unknown cards (52 minus 6 equals 46). Since there are 13 hearts in a deck of cards, and you have a four-flush, there are 9 hearts left for you to catch for the flush. That means out of the 46 unknown cards, 9 make the flush, and 37 do not (46 minus 9 equals 37). Therefore, the odds are 37 to 9 against making the flush. Another way to say this is you have 9 chances out of 46 to make the flush. In other words, the chances are just over 4-1 against you, or slightly worse than one out of five.

Suppose the game in the above situation was pot-limit hold'em, and on fourth street the opponent bet the size of the pot. Could you call on this hand? The pot odds offered you are only 2-1, because the amount in the pot is double the amount it costs you to call. For example, if there is $1000 in the pot and the opponent bets a grand, you are you are getting 2-1 pot odds on the grand it costs you to call. Since it is over 4-1 against you, this would be a bad call. In a sense, you would be making about a $500 mistake.

If there is money left to be bet after making your draw, it is possible that the money you might make after hitting the flush could justify a call, even though you were not getting the right price. We use the term "implied odds" when our calculations have included additional money we think can be won in further betting. Let us see how the "implied odds" concept can be used.

Suppose in our flush-draw case the opponent had bet only $500, half the size of the pot. Should we call now? The odds have changed. It will cost us $500 to win $1500. We are getting 3-1 money odds and are a slightly more than a 4-1 underdog, so the price is still wrong for a call, if you only look at the pot odds. But if we think there is a reasonable chance of making some money if we make the flush, it could be right to call. Even after we know how to compute the math, we still have to use other poker skills to see whether the implied odds justify a call. In this particular situation, because it is a community card type of game, the opponent will see three hearts on the board if we make our hand. He will likely be nervous at the looks of that last card. At limit play the opponent often grits his teeth and calls your bet, because the terrific pot odds he is getting means he cannot afford to fold a possible winner. At pot-limit or no-limit play, it is a lot harder to get the opponent to pay us off when we make a hand, especially when it is something as obvious as making a flush. Still, you must think about how the betting has gone to this point, who the opponent is, whether he is stuck in the game, and any other factor that could affect the implied odds. Most decisions at big-bet poker involving the odds will require both a proper knowledge of the actual odds and good judgment in assessing the implied odds.

The implied odds do not always make a call more attractive. Sometimes the real odds on a drawing hand will be worse than they first appear. For example, in our previously mentioned layout, where our holding is A♥-3♥ and the board is K♥-9♥-6♠-4♣, it is possible that we could hit the flush and still lose. Note that two of our possible flush-cards, the 6♥ and the 4♥, also pair the board. If the opponent has a set or the fitting two pair, he will fill up when we hit our flush with either of those board-pairing flush-cards. This means that we may have only seven outs instead of nine. Also, we get to lose mucho bucks if a card hits both us and the opponent.

Naturally, if we make our hand with one card still to come, the math may change drastically. There are now two betting rounds instead of one on which we may make money. There is also the possibility the opponent may redraw on the last card and beat us. This is especially important when drawing at a straight, when either a flush or a full house will beat us on the end. On the other hand, straights have a greater concealment factor, which normally enables you to get them paid off more easily than a flush or a full house.

We have used the term "implied odds" to talk about additional money beyond the present pot size that might be won or lost if we make our hand. There is another factor that must be taken into consideration when deciding whether to call a bet. By calling, we are still contending for the pot. As we know, besides making the best hand, we may also win the pot by making an uncalled bet. Our call has preserved for us the opportunity to launch a bluff. Retention of "bluffing rights" is of enormous importance at big-bet poker, and must be included when calculating whether to call the opponent.

Here is an example from no-limit hold'em of a situation where "bluffing rights" are of paramount importance. You pick up K-Q under the gun and call the blind. The small blind calls and you play a threehanded pot vs. the small and big blinds. The flop comes A-J-6 of three different suits, giving you a gutshot ten draw for a straight. The first player bets the size of the pot, the second player folds, and it is up to you. Let's say there is $30 in the pot and the bet is also $30. Should you call?

The math of the situation is there are 47 unknown cards, of which 4 give you a winner and 43 are quite likely to leave you in second place. The odds are nearly 11-1 against you. Yet the fact of the matter is a call in this type of situation is quite a reasonable play and not uncommon at big-bet poker. To see why, let's look at the deal through your opponent's eyes. He has probably got an ace with a weak kicker for his bet. With a good kicker, he may well have raised preflop. He could have flopped two pair, but it is more likely he has only one pair. For your call under the gun preflop and a subsequent call of his bet, he will think you probably have an ace with a decent-size kicker. His most likely course of action is to check on fourth street if he still has only one pair, and release his hand if you bet. This means your game plan is to call on the flop and take the pot away from him if he checks to you on fourth street. It is a sound plan against many players, even though the odds on actually making the hand are hugely unfavorable. "Bluffing rights" must be taken into consideration when weighing whether to call, if there is the possibility of more betting on the deal.

Calculating the odds with two or more cards to come is far more difficult than doing so with only one card to come. For example, after the flop in a hold'em game there are ordinarily 47 unknown cards. (The 52-card deck less the two cards in our hand and the three board-cards equals 47.) After fourth street is dealt, there will be 46 unknown cards that could come on the end. Thus the total number of card combinations for the last two cards is 47 times 46, which is 2,162. The only accurate way to calculate the odds on something such as making a flush is to count up all the card combinations that make the hand and compare it with that total-combination number of 2,162.

Here is how we find the true odds on making the flush. We make it on fourth street with 9 cards. We multiply 9 times 46 (the number of unknown cards that could come on fifth street) to give us the number 414. There are 38 cards that do not complete the flush on fourth street (the 47 unknown cards minus the 9 cards that complete the flush). To get the number of combinations that make the hand on fifth street, we multiply 38 times 9 (the number of cards that complete the flush on fifth street) which gives us 342. That number is all the card combinations that make the hand on fifth street **when we did not already have the hand on fourth street**. It is important to note why we multiplied 38 times 9 rather than 47 times 9. It only helps us to make the hand on fifth street when we have not yet made the flush. There is no bonus for making the hand on fourth street and again on fifth street. (Indeed, if we are not drawing at the nut flush, and are playing Texas hold'em rather than Omaha, it could be quite detrimental to hit a heart on both fourth and fifth street.) To get the total number of card combinations that make our flush, we add 414 and 342 to get 756. This means that the odds on making our flush are 756 out of 2,162.

Another way to say it is the odds are 1406 to 756 against us (the number 1406 is 2,162 minus 756).

As you can see, the method of computing the odds of making a draw with two cards to come is quite messy. None of us big-bet players do it at the table. Rather, we are familiar with the odds on certain situations that are quite commonplace at the form of poker we favor. All good hold'em players know they are about a 2-1 underdog to hit a flush with two cards to come.

We often use shortcuts to give us a ballpark figure that is close enough to the true odds for most poker purposes. For example, if at hold'em I have pocket aces and my opponent has a set, here is how I would get an approximate idea of my chances of helping with two cards to come. There are 45 unknown cards that could come on fourth street. (My two cards, the opponents two cards, and the three boardcards are known; 52 minus 7 gives us 45.) Of these 45 cards, only 2 help me, and 43 do not. Thus the odds on making the hand on fourth street are 43 to 2 against. That is 21.5 to 1. Since there is yet another card to come, we can take half of 21.5 which is 10.75. The approximate number I get with this method is 10.75 to 1 against me making three aces. The true figure is [(2 times 44) plus (43 times 2)] divided into 45 times 44. That number is 174 divided into 1980, which is about 11.38 to 1. As you see, in this case we got a reasonable ballpark figure for figuring the odds on making the hand with two cards to come by guessing that they were about twice as good as the odds on making the hand with one card to come.

The above method worked reasonably accurately because we were figuring the price on a **longshot**. This method is notoriously inaccurate when the draw is **not** a longshot. For example, it is obvious that a draw that is even money with one card to come will not be a cinch if there are two cards to come. In other words, a 5 percent draw with one card to come increases to almost 10 percent with two cards to come, but a 50 percent draw with one card to come does not go to anywhere near 100 percent when there are two cards to come. The right way to think about an even-money draw is about half the time you hit it on the end you already had made it on fourth street. Thus the chances rise from 50 percent with one card to come to about 75 percent with two cards to come.

As you can see, the mathematical aspect of big-bet poker is quite complex. You must acquire a feel for figuring the odds in the more common type of drawing situations. But equally important is having a feel for the implied odds of a situation, and knowing how much "bluffing rights" are worth in a particular spot. Only by taking into account all these factors can you give yourself the best chance for a successful decision.

41-PERCENTAGE TABLES
by Bob Ciaffone

The calculations in this section were made by hand. The only accurate way to do this is to list all the possible cards that could come on fourth street, and then see how many winning combinations for the drawing hand are formed with the possible fifth street cards. The number of winning combinations are added, and this sum is then divided by the total number of possible combinations (1980) to give the percentage of times the drawing hand will win. Obviously, the winning percentage for the opposing hand is found by deducting the winning percentage of the drawing hand from 100 percent.

The total number of possible combinations (1980) is formed by multiplying the number of possible fourth street cards (45) by the number of possible fifth street cards (44). The number 45 is derived by taking the total number of cards in the deck (52) and subtracting the number of cards we know (7). The cards we know are the three boardcards and the four cards that are held by the players contending the pot. It is irrelevant whether the unknown cards are in the remaining stock of the deck or in the discard pile.

As an example of the method used for these charts, here is how the calculation on a flush-draw vs. two pair was made.

flop	flush-draw	two pair
K♥-9♥-8♣	4♥-3♥	9♦-8♦

Cards	# in deck	times	5th St. Wins	equals	Combinations
♥	8	x	40	=	320
4	3	x	10	=	30
3	3	x	10	=	30
8	2	x	0	=	0
9	2	x	0	=	0
Other	27	x	8	=	216
					596 total

596 divided by 1980 equals 30.1 percent for the drawing hand, leaving 69.9 for the two pair. There are nine hearts left in the deck, but the 8♥ fills the two pair, so it is counted as a lockout card (along with the 8♠, 9♣, and 9♠). "Other" is of course any card not previously mentioned, and is derived by adding the sum of the cards previously mentioned and subtracting this figure from 45, which is the number of unknown cards on fourth street. The number of 5th street wins for each card or card grouping is based on the 44 different cards that could come on fifth street. For example, the eight hearts that could come on fourth street will win unless an 8 or 9 comes on fifth street to make the opponent a full house. There are only four cards that fill the opponent, so the remaining 40 cards will win for the draw. If a 4 or 3 hits the board on fourth street, the draw can win with eight hearts plus two cards that make trips, for a total of ten cards. Obviously, if an 8 or 9 comes on fourth street to fill the two pair hand, the draw has no wins on the last card. By adding all the cards for which we have calculated the odds, we find there are 18 in total. We subtract 18 from 45 to give us 27 cards that can come on fourth street which are neutral in character. For these 27 cards, the flush-draw will have eight cards that can come on the end that complete a flush without making the opponent a full house. In other words, every heart except the 8♥ will give the flush-draw a winning hand.

This same basic method was used for all the other calculations in this section. The number of times a drawing hand of a certain type will win can vary slightly from the figures provided in this section, which are based only on the specific hands given. For example, with a flush-draw and overcard against top pair, it would make a slight difference if the overcard were bigger or smaller than the pair's sidecard. A frequent occurrence is for the draw to have a three-flush or some sort of three-card straight working along with the main drawing combination. Naturally, a back-door possibility improves things a little bit for the draw.

ODDS FOR COMMON HOLD'EM MATCHUPS

(The percentage figure under the hand indicates how often the draw will win against that hand with two cards to come)

FLOP	DRAW	TOP PAIR	TOP TWO	TOP SET
(1) Straight-draw				
9♥-8♣-2♥	7♠-6♠	A♦-9♦	9♦-8♦	9♦-9♠
		34.2%	28.0%	25.9%
(2) Flush-draw				
K♥-Q♣-2♥	8♥-7♥	A♦-K♦	K♦-Q♦	K♦-K♠
		36.6%	30.1 %	23.4%
(3) Flush-draw + overcard				
9♥-8♣-2♥	K♥-4♥	A♦-9♦	9♦-8♦	9♦-9♠
		44.9%	31.0%	25.4%
(4) Flush-draw + two overcards				
9♥-8♣-2♥	A♥-K♥	10♦-9♦	9♦-8♦	9♦-9♠
		53.0%	31.0%	25.4%
(5) Straight-draw + overcard				
9♥-8♣-2♥	10♠-7♠	A♦-9♦	9♦-8♦	9♦-9♠
		37.0%	31.0%	25.9%
(6) Straight-draw + two overcards				
9♥-8♣-2♥	J♠-10♠	A♦-9♦	9♦-8♦	9♦-9♠
		42.1%	31.0%	25.9%
(7) Nut flush-draw + pair				
9♥-8♥-2♣	A♥-2♥	K♦-9♦	9♦-8♦	9♦-9♠
		51.2%	42.1 %	30.9%

(8) Flush-draw + overcard + gutshot

9♥-8♣-2♥	J♥-7♥	A♦-9♦	9♦-8♦	9♦-9♠
		50.2%	39.5%	33.0%

(9) Flush-draw + two overcards + gutshot

9♥-8♣-2♥	Q♥-J♥	A♦-9♦	9♦-8♦	9♦-9♠
		54%	38.4%	33.9%

(10) Flush-draw + straight-draw

9♥-8♣-2♥	7♥-6♥	A♦-9♦	9♦-8♦	9♦-9♠
		56.9%	49.2%	44.7%

ODDS FOR COMMON OMAHA MATCHUPS
(Reprinted from Bob Ciaffone's book "Omaha Holdem Poker")

(1) Set vs. Overpair and Flush-draw ... set is 1.97 favorite

Hand A	Hand B	Board
9♠ 9♦ 4♠ 4♦	A♦ A♣ J♣ 6♦	9♣ 8♥ 3♣

(2) Set vs. Gutshot Straight-draw and Flush-draw ... set is 1.91 favorite

Hand A	Hand B	Board
9♠ 9♦ 4♠ 4♦	A♣ Q♦ J♦ 6♣	9♣ 8♥ 3♣

(3) Set vs. Overpair and Straight-draw ... set is 1.88 favorite

Hand A	Hand B	Board
9♠ 9♦ 4♠ 4♦	A♠ A♦ J♠ 10♦	9♣ 8♥ 3♣

(4) Set vs. 13-Way Straight-draw ... set is 1.44 favorite

Hand A	Hand B	Board
9♠ 9♦ 4♠ 4♦	Q♥ J♣ 10♠ 2♠	9♣ 8♥ 3♣

(5) Set vs. Open-end Straight-and-Flush-draw ... set is 1.38 favorite

Hand A	Hand B	Board
9♠ 9♦ 4♠ 4♦	A♣ J♣ 10♦ 5♥	9♣ 8♥ 3♣

(6) Set vs. 17-Way Straight-draw ... set is 1.03 favorite

Hand A	Hand B	Board
9♠ 9♦ 4♠ 4♦	J♣ 10♠ 7♦ 2♥	9♣ 8♥ 3♣

(7) Set vs. 13-Way Straight-and-Flush-draw ... draw is 1.11 favorite

Hand A	Hand B	Board
9♠ 9♦ 4♠ 4♦	A♣ Q♥ J♠ 10♣	9♣ 8♥ 3♣

(8) Set vs. 20-Way Straight-draw ... draw is 1.19 favorite

Hand A	Hand B	Board
9♠ 9♦ 4♠ 4♦	J♣ 10♠ 7♥ 6♦	9♣ 8♥ 3♣

(9) Set vs. 17-Way Straight-and-Flush-draw ... draw is 1.23 favorite

Hand A	Hand B	Board
9♠ 9♦ 4♠ 4♦	J♣ 10♠ 7♥ 2♣	9♣ 8♥ 3♣

(10) Set vs. 20-Way Straight-and-Flush-draw ... draw is 1.43 favorite

Hand A	Hand B	Board
9♠ 9♦ 4♠ 4♦	J♣ 10♠ 7♥ 6♣	9♣ 8♥ 3♣

42-SPECIAL ODDS TABLES
by Stewart Reuben

PERCENTAGES AT HOLD'EM FOR TWO HANDS BEFORE THE FLOP

The third column shows the percentage of the time Hand A gets the money over Hand B when they are all-in before the flop.

HAND A	HAND B	WINS FOR HAND A
Q♣-Q♥	5♦-5♠	81%
5♦-5♠	A♠-K♠	51%
2♥-2♠	A♥-K♠	52%
K♦-Q♦	2♥-2♠	51%
J♣-J♠	A♥-10♥	67%
A♥-A♠	K♦-Q♦	82%
A♥-A♠	7♥-2♠	88%
A♥-K♠	9♦-8♦	58%
A♥-2♥	10♠-9♠	54%
A♥-10♠	A♦-9♦	67%

All-in coups before the flop, especially at no-limit, are quite common in hold'em. The above table demonstrates unequivocally, in nearly all circumstances, the winning hand before the flop is favorite over the drawing hand.

Amarillo Slim's hustling proposition has something to teach us. He will offer to wager you $1000 about the following three hands. Pair of deuces, A-K offsuit, and J-10 suited. You can choose whichever hand you like first. He chooses second. Amarillo will get the money over a number of hands. If you choose deuces, he goes for J-10 suited; if you choose J-10 suited, then he'll opt for A-K offsuit; if you go for A-K offsuit, he'll take the deuces.

We all know there is no absolute sanctuary in hold'em before the flop. Even aces against the absurd 7-2 offsuit is less than a 15-2 favorite. Our objective, when calling a raise with low cards (such as 9♦-8♦) before the flop, is that we hope to hit the flop and then win money, having made the out-draw. The low hand can walk away from the flop with no regrets; the high hand has greater difficulties.

One hand we don't want to get heavily involved with is the low pair. Either we are a tiny favorite or a massive dog. Such situations are common in poker; avoid them like the plague!

AVERAGE QUALITY OF HAND TABLE

It is constructive to know the value of hand you need for it to win the average number of hands for that number of players. This has been worked out assuming the money is all-in before the flop.

PLAYERS	%	UNSUITED CARDS	SUITED CARDS
2	50	Q-2, J-6, 10-8	J-3, 10-6, 9-7
4	25	3-3, K-5, Q-6, J-7	Q-3, J-5, 10-6, 9-7
7	14	2-2, A-3, K-5, Q-7	Q-5, J-6, 10-6, 9-7, 8-7
10	10	3-3, A-4, K-10, Q-J	Q-3, J-4, 10-5, 9-6, 8-6

This table is of limited value. In a tenhanded game, you are not going to win any medals calling with 10-5 suited before the flop in an unraised pot, unless you are solely up against the blinds. Even then, you need it to be all-in. The problems if there is betting after the flop are insuperable.

The later your position, the more information you have about the actions of the players before you. If there are two blinds and you are in Position 9, then you are in a four-handed game. Now a call with somewhat better than 10-8 is justified according to the table. Since the first six people have all passed, the three remaining hands on which you have no information yet will contain a somewhat larger proportion of high cards than the average.

PERCENTAGES IN FOUR-WAY HANDS

Again we assume the hand will be all-in.

Holecards	A♣-5♥	K♦-Q♥	J♦-10♦	8♠-7♠
Winning %	29	28	25	18

Holecards	A♣-A♦	K♥-9♥	Q♣-J♣	A♠-4♠
Winning %	68	12	13	7

Holecards	8♦-8♥	A♣-J♣	K♥-Q♦	Q♣-9♠
Winning %	29	33	25	13

Holecards	2♥-2♠	A♣-K♦	Q♠-8♠	10♥-7♥
Winning %	23	34	23	20

Holecards	A♥-Q♣	A♣-10♦	K♣-J♥	6♠-5♠
Winning %	28	16	30	26

Naturally, when any of our above hands are strong, we can increase their likelihood of standing up by betting, thus driving out weak hands which would have outdrawn us. Flopping 6♥-4♣-4♦ when holding 6♣-6♦ is a monster. It wins 92% if slowplayed. But the losing 8% is a disaster. Not only will you lose the pot, but also a bet and raise. At big-bet poker this is many times the original pot size.

We all fall in love with drawing hands. The tables show how unwise this is except when the hand holds premium overcards.

HIGH-LOW OMAHA 8-OR-BETTER PROBABILITIES

Odds Of Making A Low Taking The Hand To The River

Holding	Flop	4th St	River
A-2-3-4	13-2 (13%)	9-5 (36%)	4-5 (55%)
A-2-3-J	7-1 (12%)	2-1 (33%)	even (50%)
A-2-Q-J	12-1 (7%)	4-1 (20%)	8-5 (38%)

This tells us very little. Going all-in with A-2-3-4 offsuit against A-2-3-4 double-suited leaves you with no wins at all, just praying one of the two flushes doesn't come up. If the final board is A-2-3-4-5, then you'll be quartered off by 2-3-6. For this reason, you need A-A-2-3 or a close approximation to charge all-in before the flop. It is perfectly reasonable to raise once to clear out the fellow-travelers, but a monster is required to go to the table.

Odds Of Making A Low If The Flop Shows Two To A Low

e.g. You hold A-2-3-4 and the flop is Q-8-7

Holding	Making It 4th St	Making It 4th and/or 5th St
A 2 3 4	4-3 (43%)	1-2 (68%)
A 2 3 J	6-5 (45%)	3-7 (70%)
A 2 Q J	2-1 (34%)	3-4 (57%)

If you hold just A-2 with no high potential, then you may end up being quartered, especially if there is more than one opponent. Calling with one card to come just to make a low just isn't on. This table makes it look as if A-2-3 is a better hand than A-2-3-4. This is quite wrong. You are much more likely to make a straight or high with the four-card hand than just three cards.

OUTCOME OF TWO HANDS ALL-IN PREFLOP

With 8-6-4-2 offsuit against K-K-Q-Q double-suited, each hand will garner half the money in the long run. The low draw scoops (wins both ways) 24%, wins the low 34%, and wins high 9%. If the kings-queens hand is unsuited, the other hand wins 53% of the money.

My thanks to Dr. Mahmood Mahmood for help in deriving these figures, which are useful in shaping our strategy. Any errors are mine.

If we hold A-2-K-10 on the Q-8-7 flop, then we are only four to three against making the low. But we may end up being quartered off, especially if there is more than one opponent. Calling a bet with one card to come just isn't on.

We hope you are now convinced A-Q-9-2 isn't much to write home about. A-Q-Q-2 is superior. Here you have a high hand made. You may get three-quarters of the pot with a flop such as 8-7-3. But beware of an 8-7-2, which counterfeits your low. You may end up with neither end of it.

LONDON LOWBALL, RAZZ, & 8-OR-BETTER STUD

The statistics for the low end of it are identical for razz and eight-or-better stud, and can be compared with the London game. In London lowball, the best low is 6 4 3 2 A, as both straights and flushes count high. In razz and eight-or-better stud, a holding of 5 4 3 2 A is the monster. These latter two games are seldom played pot-limit in America, but they are in England. The chance in any of these games of starting with three to an eight-low in the first three cards is sixteen percent, about one hand in seven. The probability of making an eight-low or better at each point during the deal when starting with three unpaired low cards is given in the following table.

PROBABILITY

	London lowball	Razz or 8-or-better
By Card 5	12.6%	13.6%
By Card 5 or 6	23.7%	25.4%
By Card 5, 6 or 7	33.3%	35.6%

PROBABILITY OF MAKING AN EIGHT-LOW OR BETTER WITH CERTAIN HOLDINGS

	Razz or Eight-Or-Better	London Lowball	
	Holding 8 6 4 A	Holding 6 4 3 2	Holding 5 4 3 2
Card 5	33%	25%	17%
Card 5, 6	56%	44%	31%
Card 5, 6, 7	70%	55%	42%

PROBABILITY OPPONENT'S HAND IS FLAWED AT LONDON LOWBALL

You hold (7 4) 2 9

Opponent (? ?) 5 6	52%
Opponent (? ?) A 6	25%

We assume he started with at worst three to an 8 low. By flawed, we mean he has paired or has four to a straight (open-ended or middle-pin). If your opponent bets the pot with 5-6 here, you are doing nothing wrong raising all-in. If he bets small, he has you over a barrel. He may be extremely strong or very weak. (X A) 5 6, where X is a 2, 3, or 4, constitutes a monster against your hand.

We hope you realize four cards to a nine-low is unplayable in high-low even with no qualifier. The reason an eight-low was selected as the break-off point for establishing what is needed for a qualifier is it normally takes at least this much hand to win a pot, whether forced to by the laws of the game or not.

CONCLUSION

This is the Second Edition of our book; it is the same length as our original edition. The main change of substance is the adding of three pages to the hold'em section. This was accomplished by dropping the two-page chapter on Five-card and Six-card Omaha, and changing the hold'em quiz by substituting a problem of shorter length (but greater importance). The hold'em section now covers the differences between pot-limit hold'em and no-limit hold'em in greater depth. We have paid close attention to the comments of our original edition readers and adopted many of their suggestions. The text has been reworded throughout for greater clarity and readability. We feel the changes are insufficient to require someone who already has a copy of our book to rush out and buy the Second Edition (this would require a lot of new material), but we do think the changes have measurably improved the book, and take delight in doing so.

We hope you have enjoyed "Pot-limit And No-limit Poker." There is a wealth of technical information in it that is simply unavailable anywhere else. One time, a young professional poker player swore at Stewart after reading our book and seeing how much we revealed!

As you can see, big-bet poker is far more complex than limit poker. You have only to picture trying to write a computer program that plays poker to realize that letting the bettor select the amount wagered and allowing him to bet a large amount in relation to the money in the pot adds a much greater dimension to the game. The large increase in the skill factor gives the big-bet player an opportunity to make money, and provides much enjoyment in the playing. Frankly, it gives one the feeling that only now are you playing "real poker." Our wish is that the number of real poker players will greatly increase, so please go forth and multiply!

INDEX OF POKER PERSONALITIES